TEACHER'S PET PUBLICATIONS

PUZZLE PACK
for
Esperanza Rising

based on the book by
Pam Munoz Ryan

Written by
Mary B. Collins

© 2008 Teacher's Pet Publications
All Rights Reserved

The materials in this packet are copyrighted by Teacher's Pet Publications, Inc.

These pages may be duplicated by the purchaser for use in the purchaser's own classroom.

Copying any of these materials and distributing them for any other purpose is a violation of the copyright laws.

© 2008 Teacher's Pet Publications, Inc.
www.tpet.com

INTRODUCTION
If you already own the LitPlan for this title, this Puzzle Pack will refresh your Unit Resource Materials and Vocabulary Resource Materials sections plus give you additional materials you can substitute into the tests. If you do not already have a complete LitPlan, these pages will give you some supplemental materials to use with your own plan. There are two main groups of materials: one set for unit words (such as characters' names, symbols, places, etc.) and one set for vocabulary words associated with the book.

WORD LIST
There is a word list for both the unit words and the vocabulary words. These lists show you which words are being used in the materials and the clues or definitions being used for those words. You may want to give students a word list with clues/definitions to help them, or you may want students to only have a word list (without clues/definitions) if you want them to work a little harder. Both are available for duplication. The word lists can also be your "calling key" for the bingo games.

FILL IN THE BLANK AND MATCHING
There are 4 each of the fill in the blank and matching worksheets for both the unit and vocabulary words. These pages can be used either as extra worksheets for students or as objective parts of a unit test. They can be done individually if students need extra help or as a whole class activity to review the material covered.

MAGIC SQUARES
The magic squares not only reinforce the material covered but also work on reasoning and math skills. Many teachers have told us that their students really enjoy doing these!

WORD SEARCH PUZZLES
The word search words go in all directions, as indicated on your answer keys. Two of the word search puzzles have the clues listed rather than the words. This makes the puzzle a little more difficult, but it reinforces the material better. Two word search puzzles have words only for students who find the clue puzzles too difficult.

CROSSWORD PUZZLES
Both unit and vocabulary word sections have 4 crossword puzzles.

BINGO CARDS
There are 32 individual bingo cards for the unit words and 32 individual bingo cards for the vocabulary words. You can use your word list as a "call list," calling the words at random and marking them off of your list as you go, or you could use the flash cards by cutting them apart and drawing the words at random from a hat (or box or whatever). To make a better review, you might ask for the definition and spelling of each word as you call it out–or you could call out the definitions and have students tell you the words they need to look for on the puzzle.

JUGGLE LETTERS
The vocabulary juggle letter game is intended to help students learn the spellings of the words. One sheet has the definitions listed on it as an extra help for students who need it or to reinforce the definitions if you choose to do so.

FLASH CARDS
We've included a set of vocabulary flash cards you can duplicate, cut, and fold for your students. Some teachers make a few sets for general use by the class; others make a set for each student. Some teachers duplicate them for each student and have the students cut & fold their own. You can cut out just the words and put them in a hat, have each student pick out one word and write the definition and a sentence for that word. Students then swap words and papers, with the next student adding a sentence of his own under the last one. You can have students swap as many times as you like. Each time the student will read the sentences written prior to his own and then add a sentence. You can cut out the words and definitions separately and play "I Have; Who Has?" Each student in the room draws a word and definition. The first student says, "I have (the name of the word). Who has the definition?" The student with the definition reads it then says, "I have (the name of the vocabulary word she has). Who has the definition?" The round continues until all words and definitions have been given.

Esperanza Rising Word List

No.	Word	Clue/Definition
1.	ABUELITA	Esperanza's maternal grandmother
2.	ADA	Marta's mother
3.	AGUASCALIENTES	Location of El Rancho de las Rosas
4.	ALFONSO	Hortensia's husband; Miguel's father
5.	ANYTHING	What Isabel wants for Christmas
6.	ARVIN	Location of the camp where Esperanza and Mama live and work in California
7.	AVOCADO	Esperanza puts this on her hands to make them soft
8.	BLANKET	Esperanza has instructions to finish this while waiting for Abuelita
9.	CAMPESINOS	Field workers
10.	CARMEN	Gives Mama 2 hens; the egg lady
11.	DOLL	Papa's last gift to Esperanza
12.	EYES	Esperanza cuts these off the potatoes
13.	FIESTA	Celebrates the end of harvest & Esperanza's birthday
14.	FIRE	Destroys the Ortegas' house
15.	FLAN	Made by Josefina to sell at the jamaica
16.	GRAPES	Main crop of El Rancho de las Rosas
17.	GROTTO	Contains a statue of Our Lady of Guadalupe
18.	HORTENSIA	Esperanza's housekeeper
19.	IMMIGRATION	La Migra; sent strikers to Mexico
20.	ISABEL	Wants to be the Queen of May
21.	JAMAICAS	Summer camp parties held every Sat. night
22.	JOSEFINA	Isabel's mother
23.	JUAN	Isabel's father
24.	LAND	Esperanza can feel its heart beating.
25.	LUIS	Wants to marry Mama
26.	MARCO	Mayor of Aguascalientes
27.	MARISOL	Esperanza's best friend
28.	MARTA	Wants the workers to strike
29.	MELINA	Esperanza's new friend who helps watch the twins
30.	MIGUEL	Boy Esperanza declared she would marry one day
31.	NUNS	Abuelita's sisters who help Mama & Esperanza get their traveling papers
32.	OAXACA	Hortensia is from there.
33.	PAPA	Promised Miguel he would help him get a job on the railroad one day
34.	PATRONA	Spanish for Head of the Household
35.	PHOENIX	Metaphor Abuelita uses to describe how they will overcome troubles.
36.	PINATA	Bought for Mama but given to the campesino family
37.	PLUMS	Cause the twins to become ill
38.	POOL	Mexican workers could use it on Friday afternoons
39.	QUINCEANERA	Presentation party for girls at age 15
40.	RAILROAD	Working there is Miguel's dream job.
41.	RAMONA	Esperanza's mother
42.	REINA	Miguel's nickname for Esperanza
43.	ROSES	Brought to CA by Miguel & Alfonso as a surprise
44.	RYAN	Author of Esperanza Rising
45.	SIXTO	Esperanza's father
46.	STRIKERS	They hide dangerous surprises in the harvest.

Esperanza Rising Word List Continued

No.	Word	Clue/Definition
47.	SWEEPING	Esperanza's job when she first arrives at camp
48.	THORN	Makes Esperanza think, 'Bad luck.'
49.	TWINS	Lupe and Pepe
50.	YAKOTA	Market owner who is kind to Mexicans
51.	ZIGZAG	Pattern in Abuelita's blanket

Esperanza Rising Fill In The Blanks 1

_____ 1. Brought to CA by Miguel & Alfonso as a surprise

_____ 2. Gives Mama 2 hens; the egg lady

_____ 3. Esperanza's new friend who helps watch the twins

_____ 4. What Isabel wants for Christmas

_____ 5. Celebrates the end of harvest & Esperanza's birthday

_____ 6. Metaphor Abuelita uses to describe how they will overcome troubles.

_____ 7. Made by Josefina to sell at the jamaica

_____ 8. They hide dangerous surprises in the harvest.

_____ 9. Pattern in Abuelita's blanket

_____ 10. Esperanza's mother

_____ 11. Contains a statue of Our Lady of Guadalupe

_____ 12. Esperanza's father

_____ 13. Esperanza cuts these off the potatoes

_____ 14. Esperanza's housekeeper

_____ 15. Working there is Miguel's dream job.

_____ 16. Isabel's mother

_____ 17. Esperanza's job when she first arrives at camp

_____ 18. Hortensia is from there.

_____ 19. Main crop of El Rancho de las Rosas

_____ 20. Mexican workers could use it on Friday afternoons

Esperanza Rising Fill In The Blanks 1 Answer Key

ROSES	1. Brought to CA by Miguel & Alfonso as a surprise
CARMEN	2. Gives Mama 2 hens; the egg lady
MELINA	3. Esperanza's new friend who helps watch the twins
ANYTHING	4. What Isabel wants for Christmas
FIESTA	5. Celebrates the end of harvest & Esperanza's birthday
PHOENIX	6. Metaphor Abuelita uses to describe how they will overcome troubles.
FLAN	7. Made by Josefina to sell at the jamaica
STRIKERS	8. They hide dangerous surprises in the harvest.
ZIGZAG	9. Pattern in Abuelita's blanket
RAMONA	10. Esperanza's mother
GROTTO	11. Contains a statue of Our Lady of Guadalupe
SIXTO	12. Esperanza's father
EYES	13. Esperanza cuts these off the potatoes
HORTENSIA	14. Esperanza's housekeeper
RAILROAD	15. Working there is Miguel's dream job.
JOSEFINA	16. Isabel's mother
SWEEPING	17. Esperanza's job when she first arrives at camp
OAXACA	18. Hortensia is from there.
GRAPES	19. Main crop of El Rancho de las Rosas
POOL	20. Mexican workers could use it on Friday afternoons

Esperanza Rising Fill In The Blanks 2

_____ 1. Papa's last gift to Esperanza

_____ 2. Made by Josefina to sell at the jamaica

_____ 3. Contains a statue of Our Lady of Guadalupe

_____ 4. Wants to marry Mama

_____ 5. Presentation party for girls at age 15

_____ 6. Esperanza puts this on her hands to make them soft

_____ 7. Hortensia is from there.

_____ 8. Gives Mama 2 hens; the egg lady

_____ 9. Mayor of Aguascalientes

_____ 10. Pattern in Abuelita's blanket

_____ 11. Wants to be the Queen of May

_____ 12. Celebrates the end of harvest & Esperanza's birthday

_____ 13. Location of the camp where Esperanza and Mama live and work in California

_____ 14. Esperanza's maternal grandmother

_____ 15. Esperanza's best friend

_____ 16. Hortensia's husband; Miguel's father

_____ 17. Market owner who is kind to Mexicans

_____ 18. Makes Esperanza think, 'Bad luck.'

_____ 19. Location of El Rancho de las Rosas

_____ 20. Abuelita's sisters who help Mama & Esperanza get their traveling papers

Esperanza Rising Fill In The Blanks 2 Answer Key

DOLL	1. Papa's last gift to Esperanza
FLAN	2. Made by Josefina to sell at the jamaica
GROTTO	3. Contains a statue of Our Lady of Guadalupe
LUIS	4. Wants to marry Mama
QUINCEANERA	5. Presentation party for girls at age 15
AVOCADO	6. Esperanza puts this on her hands to make them soft
OAXACA	7. Hortensia is from there.
CARMEN	8. Gives Mama 2 hens; the egg lady
MARCO	9. Mayor of Aguascalientes
ZIGZAG	10. Pattern in Abuelita's blanket
ISABEL	11. Wants to be the Queen of May
FIESTA	12. Celebrates the end of harvest & Esperanza's birthday
ARVIN	13. Location of the camp where Esperanza and Mama live and work in California
ABUELITA	14. Esperanza's maternal grandmother
MARISOL	15. Esperanza's best friend
ALFONSO	16. Hortensia's husband; Miguel's father
YAKOTA	17. Market owner who is kind to Mexicans
THORN	18. Makes Esperanza think, 'Bad luck.'
AGUASCALIENTES	19. Location of El Rancho de las Rosas
NUNS	20. Abuelita's sisters who help Mama & Esperanza get their traveling papers

Esperanza Rising Fill In The Blanks 3

_____ 1. Makes Esperanza think, 'Bad luck.'

_____ 2. Field workers

_____ 3. Esperanza's best friend

_____ 4. Hortensia is from there.

_____ 5. Esperanza's housekeeper

_____ 6. Destroys the Ortegas' house

_____ 7. Esperanza's job when she first arrives at camp

_____ 8. Market owner who is kind to Mexicans

_____ 9. Cause the twins to become ill

_____ 10. Esperanza's father

_____ 11. Location of the camp where Esperanza and Mama live and work in California

_____ 12. Miguel's nickname for Esperanza

_____ 13. Esperanza can feel its heart beating.

_____ 14. Made by Josefina to sell at the jamaica

_____ 15. Esperanza's maternal grandmother

_____ 16. Mayor of Aguascalientes

_____ 17. Wants the workers to strike

_____ 18. Hortensia's husband; Miguel's father

_____ 19. Celebrates the end of harvest & Esperanza's birthday

_____ 20. Abuelita's sisters who help Mama & Esperanza get their traveling papers

Esperanza Rising Fill In The Blanks 3 Answer Key

THORN	1. Makes Esperanza think, 'Bad luck.'
CAMPESINOS	2. Field workers
MARISOL	3. Esperanza's best friend
OAXACA	4. Hortensia is from there.
HORTENSIA	5. Esperanza's housekeeper
FIRE	6. Destroys the Ortegas' house
SWEEPING	7. Esperanza's job when she first arrives at camp
YAKOTA	8. Market owner who is kind to Mexicans
PLUMS	9. Cause the twins to become ill
SIXTO	10. Esperanza's father
ARVIN	11. Location of the camp where Esperanza and Mama live and work in California
REINA	12. Miguel's nickname for Esperanza
LAND	13. Esperanza can feel its heart beating.
FLAN	14. Made by Josefina to sell at the jamaica
ABUELITA	15. Esperanza's maternal grandmother
MARCO	16. Mayor of Aguascalientes
MARTA	17. Wants the workers to strike
ALFONSO	18. Hortensia's husband; Miguel's father
FIESTA	19. Celebrates the end of harvest & Esperanza's birthday
NUNS	20. Abuelita's sisters who help Mama & Esperanza get their traveling papers

Esperanza Rising Fill In The Blanks 4

_____

1. Promised Miguel he would help him get a job on the railroad one day
2. Esperanza's father
3. Esperanza's mother
4. Esperanza's best friend
5. Isabel's father
6. Lupe and Pepe
7. Summer camp parties held every Sat. night
8. Main crop of El Rancho de las Rosas
9. Abuelita's sisters who help Mama & Esperanza get their traveling papers
10. Location of El Rancho de las Rosas
11. Author of Esperanza Rising
12. Boy Esperanza declared she would marry one day
13. Wants to marry Mama
14. Presentation party for girls at age 15
15. Makes Esperanza think, 'Bad luck.'
16. Working there is Miguel's dream job.
17. Pattern in Abuelita's blanket
18. Esperanza can feel its heart beating.
19. Esperanza's job when she first arrives at camp
20. Esperanza puts this on her hands to make them soft

Esperanza Rising Fill In The Blanks 4 Answer Key

PAPA	1. Promised Miguel he would help him get a job on the railroad one day
SIXTO	2. Esperanza's father
RAMONA	3. Esperanza's mother
MARISOL	4. Esperanza's best friend
JUAN	5. Isabel's father
TWINS	6. Lupe and Pepe
JAMAICAS	7. Summer camp parties held every Sat. night
GRAPES	8. Main crop of El Rancho de las Rosas
NUNS	9. Abuelita's sisters who help Mama & Esperanza get their traveling papers
AGUASCALIENTES	10. Location of El Rancho de las Rosas
RYAN	11. Author of Esperanza Rising
MIGUEL	12. Boy Esperanza declared she would marry one day
LUIS	13. Wants to marry Mama
QUINCEANERA	14. Presentation party for girls at age 15
THORN	15. Makes Esperanza think, 'Bad luck.'
RAILROAD	16. Working there is Miguel's dream job.
ZIGZAG	17. Pattern in Abuelita's blanket
LAND	18. Esperanza can feel its heart beating.
SWEEPING	19. Esperanza's job when she first arrives at camp
AVOCADO	20. Esperanza puts this on her hands to make them soft

Esperanza Rising Matching 1

___ 1. POOL   A. Miguel's nickname for Esperanza
___ 2. ALFONSO   B. Celebrates the end of harvest & Esperanza's birthday
___ 3. GRAPES   C. Hortensia's husband; Miguel's father
___ 4. NUNS   D. Boy Esperanza declared she would marry one day
___ 5. STRIKERS   E. Summer camp parties held every Sat. night
___ 6. OAXACA   F. Esperanza's new friend who helps watch the twins
___ 7. MARCO   G. Esperanza's maternal grandmother
___ 8. MIGUEL   H. Abuelita's sisters who help Mama & Esperanza get their traveling papers
___ 9. CAMPESINOS   I. Mexican workers could use it on Friday afternoons
___10. FIESTA   J. Isabel's mother
___11. ABUELITA   K. Esperanza can feel its heart beating.
___12. JOSEFINA   L. Field workers
___13. PATRONA   M. Esperanza's job when she first arrives at camp
___14. ROSES   N. La Migra; sent strikers to Mexico
___15. IMMIGRATION   O. They hide dangerous surprises in the harvest.
___16. LAND   P. Wants to marry Mama
___17. LUIS   Q. Esperanza's best friend
___18. THORN   R. Makes Esperanza think, 'Bad luck.'
___19. FLAN   S. Main crop of El Rancho de las Rosas
___20. REINA   T. Hortensia is from there.
___21. JAMAICAS   U. Contains a statue of Our Lady of Guadalupe
___22. GROTTO   V. Mayor of Aguascalientes
___23. MELINA   W. Brought to CA by Miguel & Alfonso as a surprise
___24. MARISOL   X. Made by Josefina to sell at the jamaica
___25. SWEEPING   Y. Spanish for Head of the Household

Esperanza Rising Matching 1 Answer Key

I - 1. POOL	A.	Miguel's nickname for Esperanza
C - 2. ALFONSO	B.	Celebrates the end of harvest & Esperanza's birthday
S - 3. GRAPES	C.	Hortensia's husband; Miguel's father
H - 4. NUNS	D.	Boy Esperanza declared she would marry one day
O - 5. STRIKERS	E.	Summer camp parties held every Sat. night
T - 6. OAXACA	F.	Esperanza's new friend who helps watch the twins
V - 7. MARCO	G.	Esperanza's maternal grandmother
D - 8. MIGUEL	H.	Abuelita's sisters who help Mama & Esperanza get their traveling papers
L - 9. CAMPESINOS	I.	Mexican workers could use it on Friday afternoons
B - 10. FIESTA	J.	Isabel's mother
G - 11. ABUELITA	K.	Esperanza can feel its heart beating.
J - 12. JOSEFINA	L.	Field workers
Y - 13. PATRONA	M.	Esperanza's job when she first arrives at camp
W - 14. ROSES	N.	La Migra; sent strikers to Mexico
N - 15. IMMIGRATION	O.	They hide dangerous surprises in the harvest.
K - 16. LAND	P.	Wants to marry Mama
P - 17. LUIS	Q.	Esperanza's best friend
R - 18. THORN	R.	Makes Esperanza think, 'Bad luck.'
X - 19. FLAN	S.	Main crop of El Rancho de las Rosas
A - 20. REINA	T.	Hortensia is from there.
E - 21. JAMAICAS	U.	Contains a statue of Our Lady of Guadalupe
U - 22. GROTTO	V.	Mayor of Aguascalientes
F - 23. MELINA	W.	Brought to CA by Miguel & Alfonso as a surprise
Q - 24. MARISOL	X.	Made by Josefina to sell at the jamaica
M - 25. SWEEPING	Y.	Spanish for Head of the Household

Esperanza Rising Matching 2

___ 1. SWEEPING   A. Gives Mama 2 hens; the egg lady
___ 2. ZIGZAG   B. Wants the workers to strike
___ 3. ANYTHING   C. Celebrates the end of harvest & Esperanza's birthday
___ 4. OAXACA   D. Esperanza cuts these off the potatoes
___ 5. GRAPES   E. Hortensia is from there.
___ 6. LAND   F. Makes Esperanza think, 'Bad luck.'
___ 7. SIXTO   G. Esperanza's father
___ 8. RAMONA   H. Lupe and Pepe
___ 9. FIESTA   I. Summer camp parties held every Sat. night
___ 10. NUNS   J. Esperanza can feel its heart beating.
___ 11. POOL   K. Pattern in Abuelita's blanket
___ 12. EYES   L. What Isabel wants for Christmas
___ 13. QUINCEANERA   M. Esperanza's mother
___ 14. LUIS   N. Wants to marry Mama
___ 15. CARMEN   O. Mayor of Aguascalientes
___ 16. MARCO   P. Boy Esperanza declared she would marry one day
___ 17. THORN   Q. Mexican workers could use it on Friday afternoons
___ 18. MARTA   R. Spanish for Head of the Household
___ 19. JAMAICAS   S. Esperanza's job when she first arrives at camp
___ 20. CAMPESINOS   T. Main crop of El Rancho de las Rosas
___ 21. MIGUEL   U. Marta's mother
___ 22. TWINS   V. Field workers
___ 23. ROSES   W. Brought to CA by Miguel & Alfonso as a surprise
___ 24. ADA   X. Presentation party for girls at age 15
___ 25. PATRONA   Y. Abuelita's sisters who help Mama & Esperanza get their traveling papers

Esperanza Rising Matching 2 Answer Key

S - 1. SWEEPING	A.	Gives Mama 2 hens; the egg lady
K - 2. ZIGZAG	B.	Wants the workers to strike
L - 3. ANYTHING	C.	Celebrates the end of harvest & Esperanza's birthday
E - 4. OAXACA	D.	Esperanza cuts these off the potatoes
T - 5. GRAPES	E.	Hortensia is from there.
J - 6. LAND	F.	Makes Esperanza think, 'Bad luck.'
G - 7. SIXTO	G.	Esperanza's father
M - 8. RAMONA	H.	Lupe and Pepe
C - 9. FIESTA	I.	Summer camp parties held every Sat. night
Y - 10. NUNS	J.	Esperanza can feel its heart beating.
Q - 11. POOL	K.	Pattern in Abuelita's blanket
D - 12. EYES	L.	What Isabel wants for Christmas
X - 13. QUINCEANERA	M.	Esperanza's mother
N - 14. LUIS	N.	Wants to marry Mama
A - 15. CARMEN	O.	Mayor of Aguascalientes
O - 16. MARCO	P.	Boy Esperanza declared she would marry one day
F - 17. THORN	Q.	Mexican workers could use it on Friday afternoons
B - 18. MARTA	R.	Spanish for Head of the Household
I - 19. JAMAICAS	S.	Esperanza's job when she first arrives at camp
V - 20. CAMPESINOS	T.	Main crop of El Rancho de las Rosas
P - 21. MIGUEL	U.	Marta's mother
H - 22. TWINS	V.	Field workers
W - 23. ROSES	W.	Brought to CA by Miguel & Alfonso as a surprise
U - 24. ADA	X.	Presentation party for girls at age 15
R - 25. PATRONA	Y.	Abuelita's sisters who help Mama & Esperanza get their traveling papers

Esperanza Rising Matching 3

___ 1. MELINA A. Location of El Rancho de las Rosas
___ 2. AVOCADO B. Hortensia's husband; Miguel's father
___ 3. LUIS C. Pattern in Abuelita's blanket
___ 4. PINATA D. They hide dangerous surprises in the harvest.
___ 5. PHOENIX E. Wants to be the Queen of May
___ 6. ADA F. Metaphor Abuelita uses to describe how they will overcome troubles.
___ 7. QUINCEANERA G. Esperanza can feel its heart beating.
___ 8. ABUELITA H. Brought to CA by Miguel & Alfonso as a surprise
___ 9. ALFONSO I. Main crop of El Rancho de las Rosas
___ 10. EYES J. Contains a statue of Our Lady of Guadalupe
___ 11. MARISOL K. Esperanza cuts these off the potatoes
___ 12. STRIKERS L. Wants to marry Mama
___ 13. YAKOTA M. Esperanza's maternal grandmother
___ 14. ZIGZAG N. Presentation party for girls at age 15
___ 15. AGUASCALIENTES O. Esperanza's best friend
___ 16. ARVIN P. Esperanza's new friend who helps watch the twins
___ 17. ROSES Q. Esperanza has instructions to finish this while waiting for Abuelita
___ 18. ISABEL R. Mayor of Aguascalientes
___ 19. GROTTO S. Market owner who is kind to Mexicans
___ 20. BLANKET T. Cause the twins to become ill
___ 21. GRAPES U. La Migra; sent strikers to Mexico
___ 22. LAND V. Esperanza puts this on her hands to make them soft
___ 23. MARCO W. Bought for Mama but given to the campesino family
___ 24. IMMIGRATION X. Location of the camp where Esperanza and Mama live and work in California
___ 25. PLUMS Y. Marta's mother

Esperanza Rising Matching 3 Answer Key

P - 1.	MELINA	A.	Location of El Rancho de las Rosas
V - 2.	AVOCADO	B.	Hortensia's husband; Miguel's father
L - 3.	LUIS	C.	Pattern in Abuelita's blanket
W - 4.	PINATA	D.	They hide dangerous surprises in the harvest.
F - 5.	PHOENIX	E.	Wants to be the Queen of May
Y - 6.	ADA	F.	Metaphor Abuelita uses to describe how they will overcome troubles.
N - 7.	QUINCEANERA	G.	Esperanza can feel its heart beating.
M - 8.	ABUELITA	H.	Brought to CA by Miguel & Alfonso as a surprise
B - 9.	ALFONSO	I.	Main crop of El Rancho de las Rosas
K -10.	EYES	J.	Contains a statue of Our Lady of Guadalupe
O -11.	MARISOL	K.	Esperanza cuts these off the potatoes
D -12.	STRIKERS	L.	Wants to marry Mama
S -13.	YAKOTA	M.	Esperanza's maternal grandmother
C -14.	ZIGZAG	N.	Presentation party for girls at age 15
A -15.	AGUASCALIENTES	O.	Esperanza's best friend
X -16.	ARVIN	P.	Esperanza's new friend who helps watch the twins
H -17.	ROSES	Q.	Esperanza has instructions to finish this while waiting for Abuelita
E -18.	ISABEL	R.	Mayor of Aguascalientes
J -19.	GROTTO	S.	Market owner who is kind to Mexicans
Q -20.	BLANKET	T.	Cause the twins to become ill
I -21.	GRAPES	U.	La Migra; sent strikers to Mexico
G -22.	LAND	V.	Esperanza puts this on her hands to make them soft
R -23.	MARCO	W.	Bought for Mama but given to the campesino family
U -24.	IMMIGRATION	X.	Location of the camp where Esperanza and Mama live and work in California
T -25.	PLUMS	Y.	Marta's mother

Esperanza Rising Matching 4

___ 1. TWINS
___ 2. JOSEFINA
___ 3. ROSES
___ 4. JAMAICAS
___ 5. FLAN
___ 6. HORTENSIA
___ 7. FIRE
___ 8. LUIS
___ 9. ZIGZAG
___10. NUNS
___11. DOLL
___12. AGUASCALIENTES
___13. THORN
___14. ADA
___15. BLANKET
___16. PLUMS
___17. MARTA
___18. GRAPES
___19. GROTTO
___20. ISABEL
___21. RAMONA
___22. MARISOL
___23. QUINCEANERA
___24. PINATA
___25. MARCO

A. Location of El Rancho de las Rosas
B. Lupe and Pepe
C. Makes Esperanza think, 'Bad luck.'
D. Esperanza's housekeeper
E. Isabel's mother
F. Presentation party for girls at age 15
G. Destroys the Ortegas' house
H. Abuelita's sisters who help Mama & Esperanza get their traveling papers
I. Esperanza's mother
J. Wants the workers to strike
K. Contains a statue of Our Lady of Guadalupe
L. Bought for Mama but given to the campesino family
M. Marta's mother
N. Summer camp parties held every Sat. night
O. Esperanza's best friend
P. Brought to CA by Miguel & Alfonso as a surprise
Q. Wants to marry Mama
R. Wants to be the Queen of May
S. Pattern in Abuelita's blanket
T. Made by Josefina to sell at the jamaica
U. Esperanza has instructions to finish this while waiting for Abuelita
V. Main crop of El Rancho de las Rosas
W. Mayor of Aguascalientes
X. Papa's last gift to Esperanza
Y. Cause the twins to become ill

Esperanza Rising Matching 4 Answer Key

B - 1. TWINS	A.	Location of El Rancho de las Rosas
E - 2. JOSEFINA	B.	Lupe and Pepe
P - 3. ROSES	C.	Makes Esperanza think, 'Bad luck.'
N - 4. JAMAICAS	D.	Esperanza's housekeeper
T - 5. FLAN	E.	Isabel's mother
D - 6. HORTENSIA	F.	Presentation party for girls at age 15
G - 7. FIRE	G.	Destroys the Ortegas' house
Q - 8. LUIS	H.	Abuelita's sisters who help Mama & Esperanza get their traveling papers
S - 9. ZIGZAG	I.	Esperanza's mother
H - 10. NUNS	J.	Wants the workers to strike
X - 11. DOLL	K.	Contains a statue of Our Lady of Guadalupe
A - 12. AGUASCALIENTES	L.	Bought for Mama but given to the campesino family
C - 13. THORN	M.	Marta's mother
M - 14. ADA	N.	Summer camp parties held every Sat. night
U - 15. BLANKET	O.	Esperanza's best friend
Y - 16. PLUMS	P.	Brought to CA by Miguel & Alfonso as a surprise
J - 17. MARTA	Q.	Wants to marry Mama
V - 18. GRAPES	R.	Wants to be the Queen of May
K - 19. GROTTO	S.	Pattern in Abuelita's blanket
R - 20. ISABEL	T.	Made by Josefina to sell at the jamaica
I - 21. RAMONA	U.	Esperanza has instructions to finish this while waiting for Abuelita
O - 22. MARISOL	V.	Main crop of El Rancho de las Rosas
F - 23. QUINCEANERA	W.	Mayor of Aguascalientes
L - 24. PINATA	X.	Papa's last gift to Esperanza
W - 25. MARCO	Y.	Cause the twins to become ill

Copyrighted

Esperanza Rising Magic Squares 1

Match the definition with the vocabulary word. Put your answers in the magic squares below. When your answers are correct, all columns and rows will add to the same number.

A. ARVIN
B. OAXACA
C. DOLL
D. ANYTHING
E. ALFONSO
F. FIESTA
G. ISABEL
H. MIGUEL
I. GRAPES
J. RYAN
K. HORTENSIA
L. EYES
M. CAMPESINOS
N. ZIGZAG
O. MARTA
P. PAPA

1. Pattern in Abuelita's blanket
2. Wants to be the Queen of May
3. Esperanza cuts these off the potatoes
4. Location of the camp where Esperanza and Mama live and work in California
5. Esperanza's housekeeper
6. Hortensia is from there.
7. Field workers
8. Boy Esperanza declared she would marry one day
9. Hortensia's husband; Miguel's father
10. Promised Miguel he would help him get a job on the railroad one day
11. Papa's last gift to Esperanza
12. Author of Esperanza Rising
13. What Isabel wants for Christmas
14. Main crop of El Rancho de las Rosas
15. Celebrates the end of harvest & Esperanza's birthday
16. Wants the workers to strike

A=	B=	C=	D=
E=	F=	G=	H=
I=	J=	K=	L=
M=	N=	O=	P=

Esperanza Rising Magic Squares 1 Answer Key

Match the definition with the vocabulary word. Put your answers in the magic squares below. When your answers are correct, all columns and rows will add to the same number.

A. ARVIN
B. OAXACA
C. DOLL
D. ANYTHING
E. ALFONSO
F. FIESTA
G. ISABEL
H. MIGUEL
I. GRAPES
J. RYAN
K. HORTENSIA
L. EYES
M. CAMPESINOS
N. ZIGZAG
O. MARTA
P. PAPA

1. Pattern in Abuelita's blanket
2. Wants to be the Queen of May
3. Esperanza cuts these off the potatoes
4. Location of the camp where Esperanza and Mama live and work in California
5. Esperanza's housekeeper
6. Hortensia is from there.
7. Field workers
8. Boy Esperanza declared she would marry one day
9. Hortensia's husband; Miguel's father
10. Promised Miguel he would help him get a job on the railroad one day
11. Papa's last gift to Esperanza
12. Author of Esperanza Rising
13. What Isabel wants for Christmas
14. Main crop of El Rancho de las Rosas
15. Celebrates the end of harvest & Esperanza's birthday
16. Wants the workers to strike

A=4	B=6	C=11	D=13
E=9	F=15	G=2	H=8
I=14	J=12	K=5	L=3
M=7	N=1	O=16	P=10

Esperanza Rising Magic Squares 2

Match the definition with the vocabulary word. Put your answers in the magic squares below. When your answers are correct, all columns and rows will add to the same number.

A. PLUMS
B. REINA
C. JAMAICAS
D. MARTA
E. RAMONA
F. CAMPESINOS
G. DOLL
H. MARCO
I. MIGUEL
J. FIRE
K. ALFONSO
L. NUNS
M. OAXACA
N. THORN
O. ANYTHING
P. ABUELITA

1. Hortensia is from there.
2. Field workers
3. Mayor of Aguascalientes
4. What Isabel wants for Christmas
5. Abuelita's sisters who help Mama & Esperanza get their traveling papers
6. Summer camp parties held every Sat. night
7. Cause the twins to become ill
8. Destroys the Ortegas' house
9. Hortensia's husband; Miguel's father
10. Wants the workers to strike
11. Miguel's nickname for Esperanza
12. Boy Esperanza declared she would marry one day
13. Makes Esperanza think, 'Bad luck.'
14. Esperanza's mother
15. Papa's last gift to Esperanza
16. Esperanza's maternal grandmother

A=	B=	C=	D=
E=	F=	G=	H=
I=	J=	K=	L=
M=	N=	O=	P=

Esperanza Rising Magic Squares 2 Answer Key

Match the definition with the vocabulary word. Put your answers in the magic squares below. When your answers are correct, all columns and rows will add to the same number.

- A. PLUMS
- B. REINA
- C. JAMAICAS
- D. MARTA
- E. RAMONA
- F. CAMPESINOS
- G. DOLL
- H. MARCO
- I. MIGUEL
- J. FIRE
- K. ALFONSO
- L. NUNS
- M. OAXACA
- N. THORN
- O. ANYTHING
- P. ABUELITA

1. Hortensia is from there.
2. Field workers
3. Mayor of Aguascalientes
4. What Isabel wants for Christmas
5. Abuelita's sisters who help Mama & Esperanza get their traveling papers
6. Summer camp parties held every Sat. night
7. Cause the twins to become ill
8. Destroys the Ortegas' house
9. Hortensia's husband; Miguel's father
10. Wants the workers to strike
11. Miguel's nickname for Esperanza
12. Boy Esperanza declared she would marry one day
13. Makes Esperanza think, 'Bad luck.'
14. Esperanza's mother
15. Papa's last gift to Esperanza
16. Esperanza's maternal grandmother

A=7	B=11	C=6	D=10
E=14	F=2	G=15	H=3
I=12	J=8	K=9	L=5
M=1	N=13	O=4	P=16

Esperanza Rising Magic Squares 3

Match the definition with the vocabulary word. Put your answers in the magic squares below. When your answers are correct, all columns and rows will add to the same number.

A. GRAPES
B. LAND
C. QUINCEANERA
D. OAXACA
E. BLANKET
F. MARCO
G. FLAN
H. DOLL
I. CAMPESINOS
J. MARTA
K. YAKOTA
L. GROTTO
M. RAILROAD
N. PAPA
O. SWEEPING
P. ARVIN

1. Presentation party for girls at age 15
2. Wants the workers to strike
3. Mayor of Aguascalientes
4. Esperanza's job when she first arrives at camp
5. Location of the camp where Esperanza and Mama live and work in California
6. Esperanza has instructions to finish this while waiting for Abuelita
7. Field workers
8. Hortensia is from there.
9. Working there is Miguel's dream job.
10. Papa's last gift to Esperanza
11. Contains a statue of Our Lady of Guadalupe
12. Main crop of El Rancho de las Rosas
13. Esperanza can feel its heart beating.
14. Market owner who is kind to Mexicans
15. Made by Josefina to sell at the jamaica
16. Promised Miguel he would help him get a job on the railroad one day

A=	B=	C=	D=
E=	F=	G=	H=
I=	J=	K=	L=
M=	N=	O=	P=

Esperanza Rising Magic Squares 3 Answer Key

Match the definition with the vocabulary word. Put your answers in the magic squares below. When your answers are correct, all columns and rows will add to the same number.

A. GRAPES
B. LAND
C. QUINCEANERA
D. OAXACA
E. BLANKET
F. MARCO
G. FLAN
H. DOLL
I. CAMPESINOS
J. MARTA
K. YAKOTA
L. GROTTO
M. RAILROAD
N. PAPA
O. SWEEPING
P. ARVIN

1. Presentation party for girls at age 15
2. Wants the workers to strike
3. Mayor of Aguascalientes
4. Esperanza's job when she first arrives at camp
5. Location of the camp where Esperanza and Mama live and work in California
6. Esperanza has instructions to finish this while waiting for Abuelita
7. Field workers
8. Hortensia is from there.
9. Working there is Miguel's dream job.
10. Papa's last gift to Esperanza
11. Contains a statue of Our Lady of Guadalupe
12. Main crop of El Rancho de las Rosas
13. Esperanza can feel its heart beating.
14. Market owner who is kind to Mexicans
15. Made by Josefina to sell at the jamaica
16. Promised Miguel he would help him get a job on the railroad one day

A=12	B=13	C=1	D=8
E=6	F=3	G=15	H=10
I=7	J=2	K=14	L=11
M=9	N=16	O=4	P=5

Esperanza Rising Magic Squares 4

Match the definition with the vocabulary word. Put your answers in the magic squares below. When your answers are correct, all columns and rows will add to the same number.

A. PHOENIX
B. AVOCADO
C. ADA
D. LAND
E. ARVIN
F. SWEEPING
G. BLANKET
H. AGUASCALIENTES
I. PAPA
J. QUINCEANERA
K. ABUELITA
L. NUNS
M. GROTTO
N. JOSEFINA
O. MARTA
P. MELINA

1. Esperanza's job when she first arrives at camp
2. Promised Miguel he would help him get a job on the railroad one day
3. Wants the workers to strike
4. Esperanza can feel its heart beating.
5. Contains a statue of Our Lady of Guadalupe
6. Esperanza puts this on her hands to make them soft
7. Location of El Rancho de las Rosas
8. Esperanza's maternal grandmother
9. Marta's mother
10. Esperanza's new friend who helps watch the twins
11. Presentation party for girls at age 15
12. Location of the camp where Esperanza and Mama live and work in California
13. Abuelita's sisters who help Mama & Esperanza get their traveling papers
14. Esperanza has instructions to finish this while waiting for Abuelita
15. Metaphor Abuelita uses to describe how they will overcome troubles.
16. Isabel's mother

A=	B=	C=	D=
E=	F=	G=	H=
I=	J=	K=	L=
M=	N=	O=	P=

Esperanza Rising Magic Squares 4 Answer Key

Match the definition with the vocabulary word. Put your answers in the magic squares below. When your answers are correct, all columns and rows will add to the same number.

A. PHOENIX
B. AVOCADO
C. ADA
D. LAND
E. ARVIN
F. SWEEPING
G. BLANKET
H. AGUASCALIENTES
I. PAPA
J. QUINCEANERA
K. ABUELITA
L. NUNS
M. GROTTO
N. JOSEFINA
O. MARTA
P. MELINA

1. Esperanza's job when she first arrives at camp
2. Promised Miguel he would help him get a job on the railroad one day
3. Wants the workers to strike
4. Esperanza can feel its heart beating.
5. Contains a statue of Our Lady of Guadalupe
6. Esperanza puts this on her hands to make them soft
7. Location of El Rancho de las Rosas
8. Esperanza's maternal grandmother
9. Marta's mother
10. Esperanza's new friend who helps watch the twins
11. Presentation party for girls at age 15
12. Location of the camp where Esperanza and Mama live and work in California
13. Abuelita's sisters who help Mama & Esperanza get their traveling papers
14. Esperanza has instructions to finish this while waiting for Abuelita
15. Metaphor Abuelita uses to describe how they will overcome troubles.
16. Isabel's mother

A=15	B=6	C=9	D=4
E=12	F=1	G=14	H=7
I=2	J=11	K=8	L=13
M=5	N=16	O=3	P=10

Esperanza Rising Word Search 1

```
Q C J P J M S T M X T J R B D T L V
U A A A M O X I B I W W C O E T U G
I R M T I Q S W X S G P I K S P I O
N M A R J S R E Z T J U N N J E S T
C E I O F L A N F A O A E O S N S W
E N C N M T R B P I L H D L O B X W
A S A A S Q D A E B N A Z F D D P Y
N D S E D R P C M L C A L G A R I A
E G I R L H J R W O F A N R O R N M
R F G M Y N U S V D N I W A R I A J
A B R A D A A M N Y A R P L R T K
G H O R T E N S I A D A R E I N A S
S D T C L I L L K L R D M S A N M S
Q F T O V V L O R N Y T O V R U E K
T H O R N O T N U N S L A Z L Y K F
Z P A S D A P H O E N I X P E P H K
```

Abuelita's sisters who help Mama & Esperanza get their traveling papers (4)
Author of Esperanza Rising (4)
Bought for Mama but given to the campesino family (6)
Boy Esperanza declared she would marry one day (6)
Brought to CA by Miguel & Alfonso as a surprise (5)
Cause the twins to become ill (5)
Celebrates the end of harvest & Esperanza's birthday (6)
Contains a statue of Our Lady of Guadalupe (6)
Destroys the Ortegas' house (4)
Esperanza can feel its heart beating. (4)
Esperanza cuts these off the potatoes (4)
Esperanza has instructions to finish this while waiting for Abuelita (7)
Esperanza puts this on her hands to make them soft (7)
Esperanza's best friend (7)
Esperanza's father (5)
Esperanza's housekeeper (9)
Esperanza's mother (6)
Esperanza's new friend who helps watch the twins (6)
Gives Mama 2 hens; the egg lady (6)

Hortensia's husband; Miguel's father (7)
Isabel's father (4)
Isabel's mother (8)
Location of the camp where Esperanza and Mama live and work in California (5)
Lupe and Pepe (5)
Made by Josefina to sell at the jamaica (4)
Main crop of El Rancho de las Rosas (6)
Makes Esperanza think, 'Bad luck.' (5)
Market owner who is kind to Mexicans (6)
Marta's mother (3)
Mayor of Aguascalientes (5)
Metaphor Abuelita uses to describe how they will overcome troubles. (7)
Mexican workers could use it on Friday afternoons (4)
Miguel's nickname for Esperanza (5)
Papa's last gift to Esperanza (4)
Presentation party for girls at age 15 (11)
Promised Miguel he would help him get a job on the railroad one day (4)
Spanish for Head of the Household (7)
Summer camp parties held every Sat. night (8)
Wants the workers to strike (5)
Wants to be the Queen of May (6)
Wants to marry Mama (4)
Working there is Miguel's dream job. (8)

Esperanza Rising Word Search 1 Answer Key

```
Q C J P   J   S   M   T   R   T L
U A A A   O   I   W   O E   U
I R M T I S   X   G   I K S   I O
N M A R S E   T   U N N   E S
C E I O F L A N F A O A E O S N S
E N C N   T R B P I L   D L O
A   A A S   A E B N A   F D   P
N   S E   P   M L C A L   R O   I A
E   I R   J   O F A   A O   N M
R F G M Y   U   V D N I   A R I A
A   R A   A A M N Y A R P L R T
  H O R T E N S I A D A R E I N A S
    T C L I   L K L R   M S A   M S
    T O V   L O     T O   R U E
T H O R N O T N U N S L A   L Y
  P A   D A P H O E N I X P E
```

Abuelita's sisters who help Mama & Esperanza get their traveling papers (4)
Author of Esperanza Rising (4)
Bought for Mama but given to the campesino family (6)
Boy Esperanza declared she would marry one day (6)
Brought to CA by Miguel & Alfonso as a surprise (5)
Cause the twins to become ill (5)
Celebrates the end of harvest & Esperanza's birthday (6)
Contains a statue of Our Lady of Guadalupe (6)
Destroys the Ortegas' house (4)
Esperanza can feel its heart beating. (4)
Esperanza cuts these off the potatoes (4)
Esperanza has instructions to finish this while waiting for Abuelita (7)
Esperanza puts this on her hands to make them soft (7)
Esperanza's best friend (7)
Esperanza's father (5)
Esperanza's housekeeper (9)
Esperanza's mother (6)
Esperanza's new friend who helps watch the twins (6)
Gives Mama 2 hens; the egg lady (6)
Hortensia's husband; Miguel's father (7)
Isabel's father (4)
Isabel's mother (8)
Location of the camp where Esperanza and Mama live and work in California (5)
Lupe and Pepe (5)
Made by Josefina to sell at the jamaica (4)
Main crop of El Rancho de las Rosas (6)
Makes Esperanza think, 'Bad luck.' (5)
Market owner who is kind to Mexicans (6)
Marta's mother (3)
Mayor of Aguascalientes (5)
Metaphor Abuelita uses to describe how they will overcome troubles. (7)
Mexican workers could use it on Friday afternoons (4)
Miguel's nickname for Esperanza (5)
Papa's last gift to Esperanza (4)
Presentation party for girls at age 15 (11)
Promised Miguel he would help him get a job on the railroad one day (4)
Spanish for Head of the Household (7)
Summer camp parties held every Sat. night (8)
Wants the workers to strike (5)
Wants to be the Queen of May (6)
Wants to marry Mama (4)
Working there is Miguel's dream job. (8)

Esperanza Rising Word Search 2

```
M S W E E P I N G N I H T Y N A B N
A Z Z G M Y M X R R A N O M A R T H
R V Z I X I F N C O P G R A P E S R
I N X M G H G H D H S O D Y X N F V
S M U L P Z O U D T X E O C A A H Z
O D A C O V A R E V J H S L N E C R
L G R O T T O G T L U Z F V B C D A
S Y N N M C B X S E A O A T A N I P
P A Y K E P A T R O N A T L U I S Q
H K H B L P Y E D S A S L W N U N R
V O F H I H B K O T X O I N I Q U J
M T D L N O P N R Q D B Y A V N N X
L A N D A E C A R M E N F I R E S W
Q N R D J N M L P Y X D J F A Y S C
R V A C B I R B D A A S A N I E R C
Q V X J O X S I X T O N F I E S T A
```

Abuelita's sisters who help Mama & Esperanza get their traveling papers (4)
Author of Esperanza Rising (4)
Bought for Mama but given to the campesino family (6)
Boy Esperanza declared she would marry one day (6)
Brought to CA by Miguel & Alfonso as a surprise (5)
Cause the twins to become ill (5)
Celebrates the end of harvest & Esperanza's birthday (6)
Contains a statue of Our Lady of Guadalupe (6)
Destroys the Ortegas' house (4)
Esperanza can feel its heart beating. (4)
Esperanza cuts these off the potatoes (4)
Esperanza has instructions to finish this while waiting for Abuelita (7)
Esperanza puts this on her hands to make them soft (7)
Esperanza's best friend (7)
Esperanza's father (5)
Esperanza's housekeeper (9)
Esperanza's job when she first arrives at camp (8)
Esperanza's mother (6)
Esperanza's new friend who helps watch the twins (6)
Gives Mama 2 hens; the egg lady (6)
Hortensia is from there. (6)
Hortensia's husband; Miguel's father (7)
Isabel's father (4)
Location of the camp where Esperanza and Mama live and work in California (5)
Lupe and Pepe (5)
Made by Josefina to sell at the jamaica (4)
Main crop of El Rancho de las Rosas (6)
Makes Esperanza think, 'Bad luck.' (5)
Market owner who is kind to Mexicans (6)
Marta's mother (3)
Mayor of Aguascalientes (5)
Metaphor Abuelita uses to describe how they will overcome troubles. (7)
Mexican workers could use it on Friday afternoons (4)
Miguel's nickname for Esperanza (5)
Papa's last gift to Esperanza (4)
Pattern in Abuelita's blanket (6)
Presentation party for girls at age 15 (11)
Promised Miguel he would help him get a job on the railroad one day (4)
Spanish for Head of the Household (7)
Wants the workers to strike (5)
Wants to marry Mama (4)
What Isabel wants for Christmas (8)

Esperanza Rising Word Search 2 Answer Key

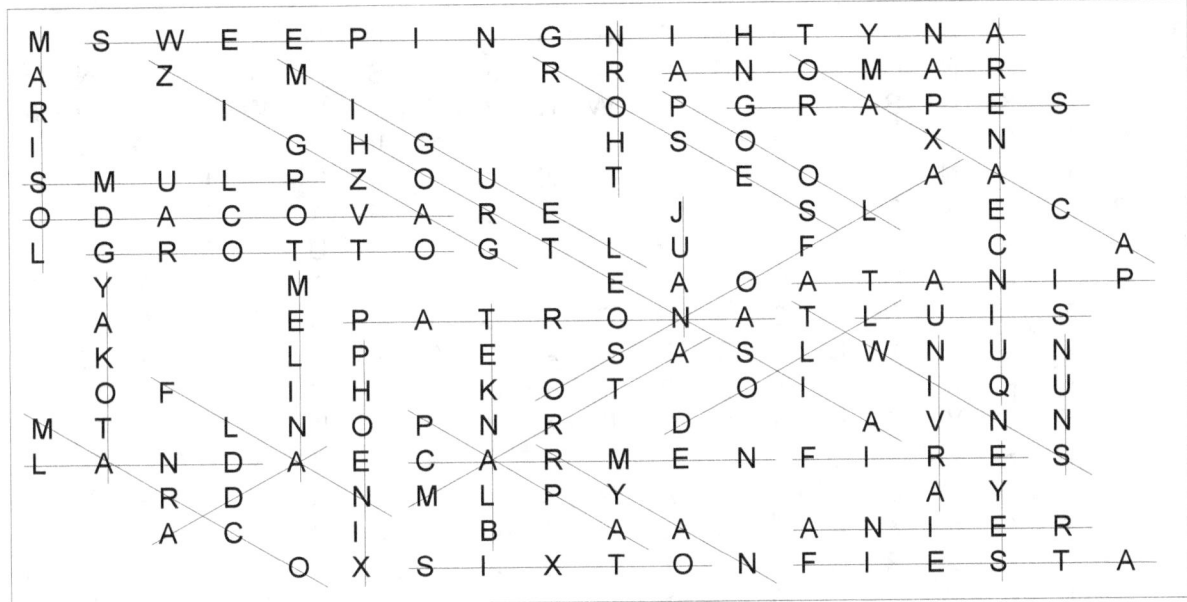

Abuelita's sisters who help Mama & Esperanza get their traveling papers (4)
Author of Esperanza Rising (4)
Bought for Mama but given to the campesino family (6)
Boy Esperanza declared she would marry one day (6)
Brought to CA by Miguel & Alfonso as a surprise (5)
Cause the twins to become ill (5)
Celebrates the end of harvest & Esperanza's birthday (6)
Contains a statue of Our Lady of Guadalupe (6)
Destroys the Ortegas' house (4)
Esperanza can feel its heart beating. (4)
Esperanza cuts these off the potatoes (4)
Esperanza has instructions to finish this while waiting for Abuelita (7)
Esperanza puts this on her hands to make them soft (7)
Esperanza's best friend (7)
Esperanza's father (5)
Esperanza's housekeeper (9)
Esperanza's job when she first arrives at camp (8)
Esperanza's mother (6)
Esperanza's new friend who helps watch the twins (6)
Gives Mama 2 hens; the egg lady (6)
Hortensia is from there. (6)
Hortensia's husband; Miguel's father (7)
Isabel's father (4)
Location of the camp where Esperanza and Mama live and work in California (5)
Lupe and Pepe (5)
Made by Josefina to sell at the jamaica (4)
Main crop of El Rancho de las Rosas (6)
Makes Esperanza think, 'Bad luck.' (5)
Market owner who is kind to Mexicans (6)
Marta's mother (3)
Mayor of Aguascalientes (5)
Metaphor Abuelita uses to describe how they will overcome troubles. (7)
Mexican workers could use it on Friday afternoons (4)
Miguel's nickname for Esperanza (5)
Papa's last gift to Esperanza (4)
Pattern in Abuelita's blanket (6)
Presentation party for girls at age 15 (11)
Promised Miguel he would help him get a job on the railroad one day (4)
Spanish for Head of the Household (7)
Wants the workers to strike (5)
Wants to marry Mama (4)
What Isabel wants for Christmas (8)

Esperanza Rising Word Search 3

```
A V O C A D O P H O E N I X F M A R T A
D L T A N C A M P E I N O S N B L A N
O F F K N S J M P R W N Y P O K W I J N
L M B O E Y C P D E F E Z P M I M S Q C Q
L T N P N R T K A R E N A E C N I U Q S
K P A L J S I H T T P R D L E A A X Y S
N R N U Q R O V I R I M T T F U F T B B
G M A M T D J V P N W R Y Z J H A A W
G E T S J D X O V H G O D W M S T H A P
I L I G W M B X S Z H A V G V O R J N B
S I L F I G Z T D E O K J C K D A H O Q
A N E G W R I B W R F X X A K K T T R O
B A U F W X G F L I V I Y R M Z S X T J
E E B W O L Z I P A N C N Y P A E A X
L G A C A X A O N U N S D A R V I N P F
J U R A L R G N M P E K P N E S F C K H
F A I O D C E D D S M A E F I F P T A P
M I X S T A D Y O Y R K T T N R O H T S
V G R W N T J R E D A B L J A W O L R C
J K F E K L O X W S C F L A N R L G C T
```

ABUELITA	FIRE	MARTA	RAILROAD
ADA	FLAN	MELINA	RAMONA
ALFONSO	GRAPES	MIGUEL	REINA
ANYTHING	GROTTO	NUNS	ROSES
ARVIN	HORTENSIA	OAXACA	RYAN
AVOCADO	ISABEL	PAPA	SIXTO
BLANKET	JAMAICAS	PATRONA	STRIKERS
CAMPESINOS	JOSEFINA	PHOENIX	SWEEPING
CARMEN	JUAN	PINATA	THORN
DOLL	LAND	PLUMS	TWINS
EYES	LUIS	POOL	YAKOTA
FIESTA	MARCO	QUINCEANERA	ZIGZAG

Esperanza Rising Word Search 3 Answer Key

ABUELITA	FIRE	MARTA	RAILROAD
ADA	FLAN	MELINA	RAMONA
ALFONSO	GRAPES	MIGUEL	REINA
ANYTHING	GROTTO	NUNS	ROSES
ARVIN	HORTENSIA	OAXACA	RYAN
AVOCADO	ISABEL	PAPA	SIXTO
BLANKET	JAMAICAS	PATRONA	STRIKERS
CAMPESINOS	JOSEFINA	PHOENIX	SWEEPING
CARMEN	JUAN	PINATA	THORN
DOLL	LAND	PLUMS	TWINS
EYES	LUIS	POOL	YAKOTA
FIESTA	MARCO	QUINCEANERA	ZIGZAG

Esperanza Rising Word Search 4

```
J X K P C A R M E N H O R T E N S I A T
A A R V I N K Y X C H D M A R I S O L Q
M Q M B Q N J S M N R O T C R E Q R A M V
A C B W T F A E V L B L R W R A X V F X
I M M I G R A T I O N L G X I N E O H P
C Y B N W T H N A Y L X A L F N W C Q B
A D R N U O L E Z M E D R N G W S A U F
S D Y D R N X I E C B O J A K R V D I N
K N A N A W S L S R A M O N A E A O N K
D P N N F M I A I D S M A I H V T P C T
C L I K U N O C X Z I L P F Y W O R E S
D E R L A S A S T I F P R E K A K O A S
R A P A P W X A O G Z L O S S T A S N X
V G A T V E A U F Z M M R O L I Y E E P
G L L P M E C G Q A W E Q J L L N S R C
L R F Z Q P A A R G K C G L M E A O A Q
X Z O L U I S T F I E S T A S U U E S J
T N N T D N A S R X K Q R N F B J Y R C
Q D S T T G D T V R H C C D D A F E R W
V F O P W O S X A N O R T A P S M S M R
```

ABUELITA	IMMIGRATION	PLUMS
ADA	ISABEL	POOL
AGUASCALIENTES	JAMAICAS	QUINCEANERA
ALFONSO	JOSEFINA	RAILROAD
ARVIN	JUAN	RAMONA
AVOCADO	LAND	REINA
BLANKET	LUIS	ROSES
CAMPESINOS	MARCO	RYAN
CARMEN	MARISOL	SIXTO
DOLL	MARTA	STRIKERS
EYES	MELINA	SWEEPING
FIESTA	NUNS	THORN
FIRE	OAXACA	TWINS
FLAN	PAPA	YAKOTA
GRAPES	PATRONA	ZIGZAG
GROTTO	PHOENIX	
HORTENSIA	PINATA	

Esperanza Rising Word Search 4 Answer Key

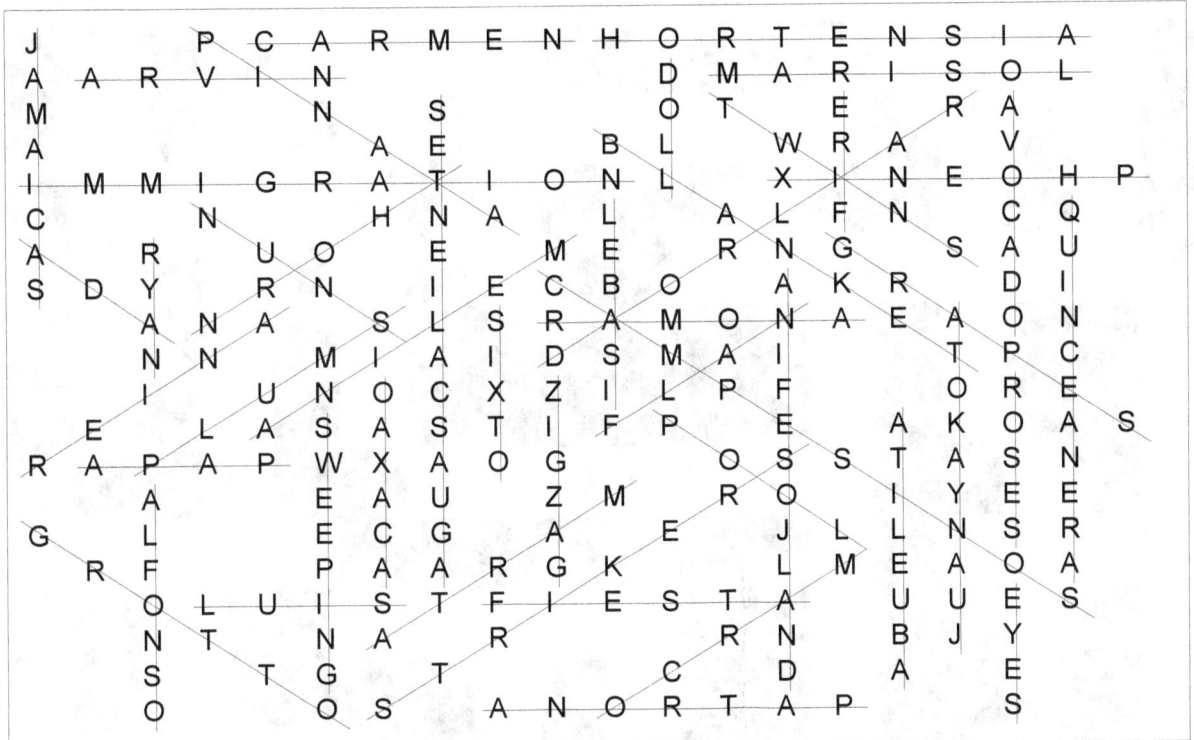

ABUELITA	IMMIGRATION	PLUMS
ADA	ISABEL	POOL
AGUASCALIENTES	JAMAICAS	QUINCEANERA
ALFONSO	JOSEFINA	RAILROAD
ARVIN	JUAN	RAMONA
AVOCADO	LAND	REINA
BLANKET	LUIS	ROSES
CAMPESINOS	MARCO	RYAN
CARMEN	MARISOL	SIXTO
DOLL	MARTA	STRIKERS
EYES	MELINA	SWEEPING
FIESTA	NUNS	THORN
FIRE	OAXACA	TWINS
FLAN	PAPA	YAKOTA
GRAPES	PATRONA	ZIGZAG
GROTTO	PHOENIX	
HORTENSIA	PINATA	

Esperanza Rising Crossword 1

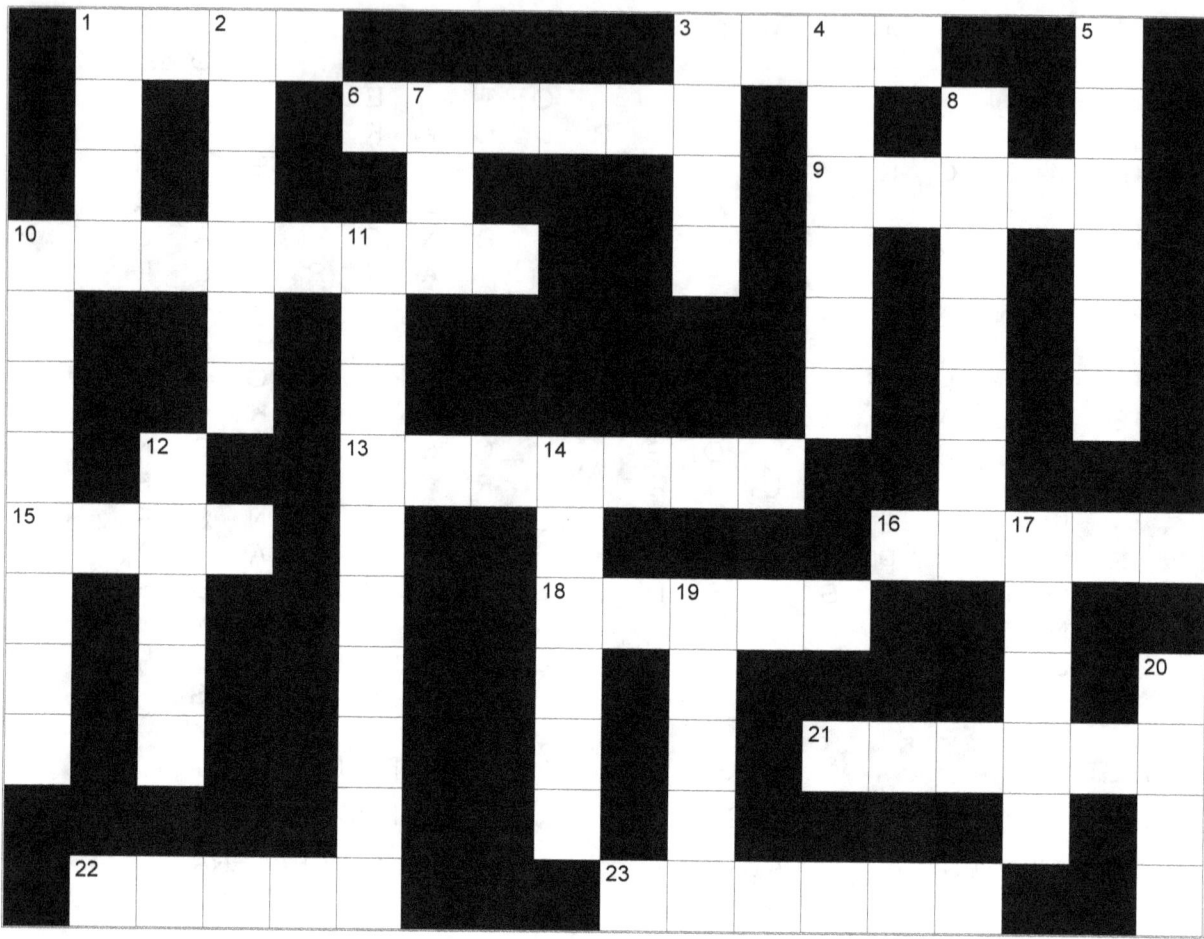

Across
1. Mexican workers could use it on Friday afternoons
3. Wants to marry Mama
6. Market owner who is kind to Mexicans
9. Location of the camp where Esperanza and Mama live and work in California
10. Summer camp parties held every Sat. night
13. Spanish for Head of the Household
15. Made by Josefina to sell at the jamaica
16. Brought to CA by Miguel & Alfonso as a surprise
18. Mayor of Aguascalientes
21. Contains a statue of Our Lady of Guadalupe
22. Lupe and Pepe
23. Gives Mama 2 hens; the egg lady

Down
1. Promised Miguel he would help him get a job on the railroad one day
2. Hortensia is from there.
3. Esperanza can feel its heart beating.
4. Wants to be the Queen of May
5. Bought for Mama but given to the campesino family
7. Marta's mother
8. Esperanza puts this on her hands to make them soft
10. Isabel's mother
11. Field workers
12. Wants the workers to strike
14. Esperanza's mother
17. Esperanza's father
19. Miguel's nickname for Esperanza
20. Papa's last gift to Esperanza

Esperanza Rising Crossword 1 Answer Key

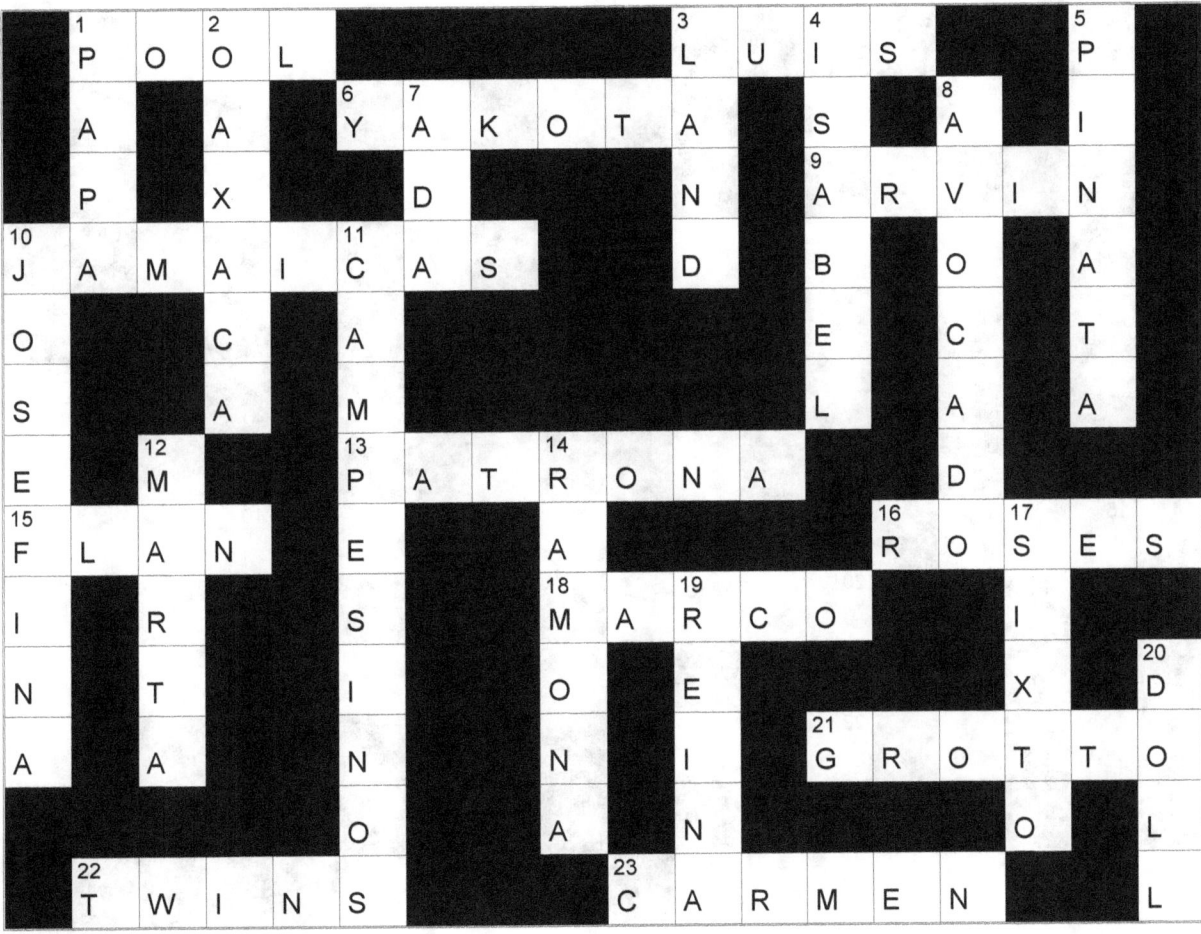

Across
1. Mexican workers could use it on Friday afternoons
3. Wants to marry Mama
6. Market owner who is kind to Mexicans
9. Location of the camp where Esperanza and Mama live and work in California
10. Summer camp parties held every Sat. night
13. Spanish for Head of the Household
15. Made by Josefina to sell at the jamaica
16. Brought to CA by Miguel & Alfonso as a surprise
18. Mayor of Aguascalientes
21. Contains a statue of Our Lady of Guadalupe
22. Lupe and Pepe
23. Gives Mama 2 hens; the egg lady

Down
1. Promised Miguel he would help him get a job on the railroad one day
2. Hortensia is from there.
3. Esperanza can feel its heart beating.
4. Wants to be the Queen of May
5. Bought for Mama but given to the campesino family
7. Marta's mother
8. Esperanza puts this on her hands to make them soft
10. Isabel's mother
11. Field workers
12. Wants the workers to strike
14. Esperanza's mother
17. Esperanza's father
19. Miguel's nickname for Esperanza
20. Papa's last gift to Esperanza

Esperanza Rising Crossword 2

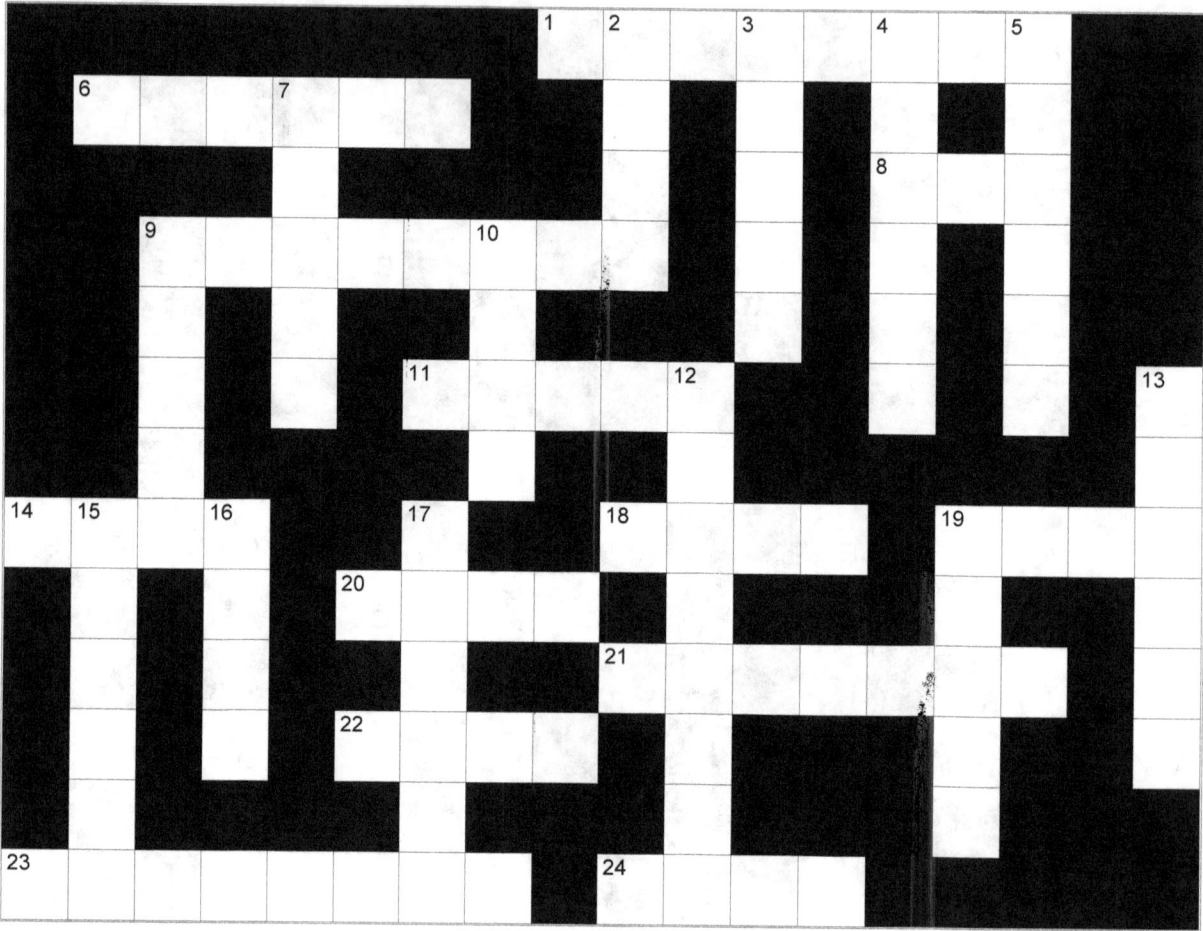

Across
1. What Isabel wants for Christmas
6. Gives Mama 2 hens; the egg lady
8. Marta's mother
9. They hide dangerous surprises in the harvest.
11. Miguel's nickname for Esperanza
14. Mexican workers could use it on Friday afternoons
18. Isabel's father
19. Author of Esperanza Rising
20. Promised Miguel he would help him get a job on the railroad one day
21. Hortensia's husband; Miguel's father
22. Papa's last gift to Esperanza
23. Summer camp parties held every Sat. night
24. Esperanza can feel its heart beating.

Down
2. Abuelita's sisters who help Mama & Esperanza get their traveling papers
3. Lupe and Pepe
4. Wants to be the Queen of May
5. Main crop of El Rancho de las Rosas
7. Wants the workers to strike
9. Esperanza's father
10. Esperanza cuts these off the potatoes
12. Esperanza's maternal grandmother
13. Bought for Mama but given to the campesino family
15. Hortensia is from there.
16. Wants to marry Mama
17. Market owner who is kind to Mexicans
19. Brought to CA by Miguel & Alfonso as a surprise

Esperanza Rising Crossword 2 Answer Key

Across
1. What Isabel wants for Christmas
6. Gives Mama 2 hens; the egg lady
8. Marta's mother
9. They hide dangerous surprises in the harvest.
11. Miguel's nickname for Esperanza
14. Mexican workers could use it on Friday afternoons
18. Isabel's father
19. Author of Esperanza Rising
20. Promised Miguel he would help him get a job on the railroad one day
21. Hortensia's husband; Miguel's father
22. Papa's last gift to Esperanza
23. Summer camp parties held every Sat. night
24. Esperanza can feel its heart beating.

Down
2. Abuelita's sisters who help Mama & Esperanza get their traveling papers
3. Lupe and Pepe
4. Wants to be the Queen of May
5. Main crop of El Rancho de las Rosas
7. Wants the workers to strike
9. Esperanza's father
10. Esperanza cuts these off the potatoes
12. Esperanza's maternal grandmother
13. Bought for Mama but given to the campesino family
15. Hortensia is from there.
16. Wants to marry Mama
17. Market owner who is kind to Mexicans
19. Brought to CA by Miguel & Alfonso as a surprise

Esperanza Rising Crossword 3

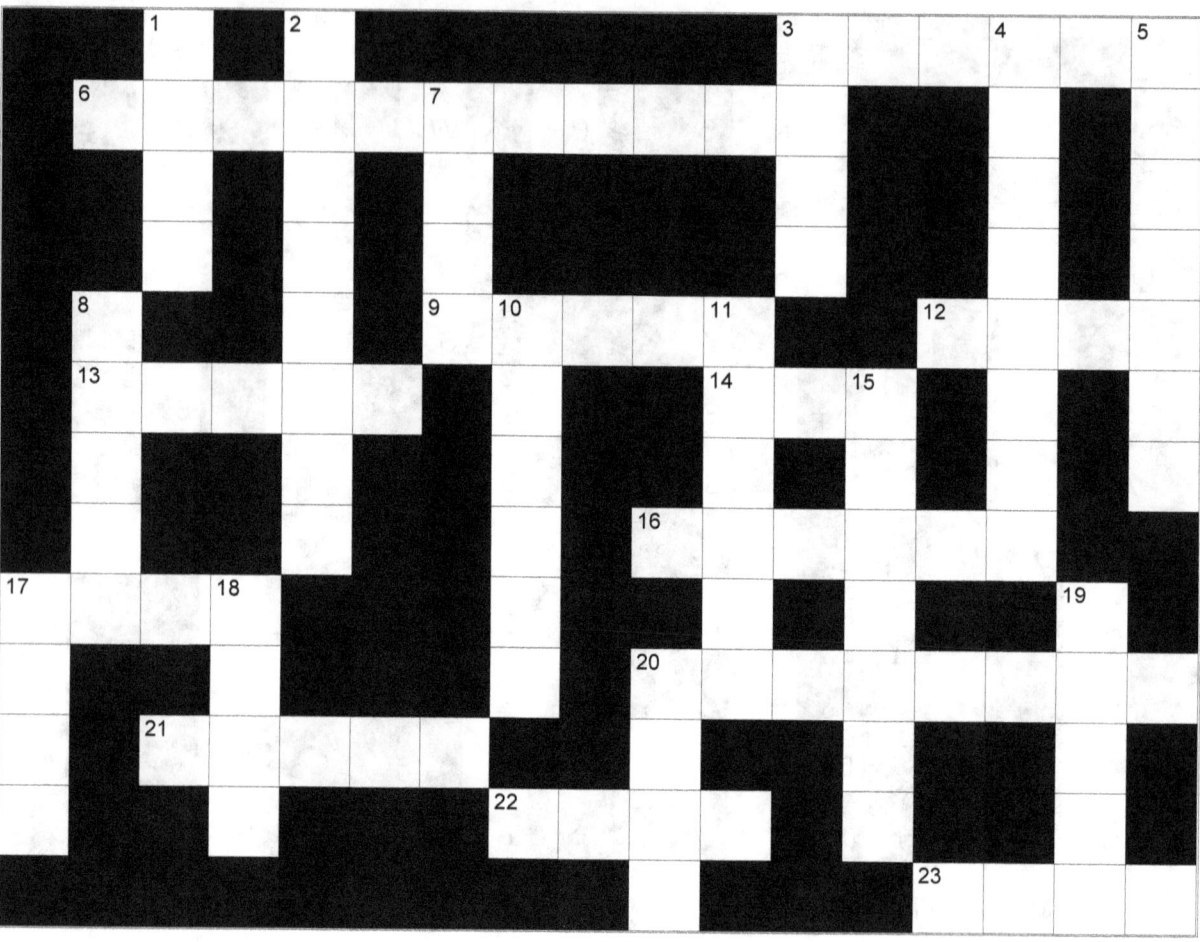

Across

3. Bought for Mama but given to the campesino family
6. Presentation party for girls at age 15
9. Esperanza's father
12. Made by Josefina to sell at the jamaica
13. Location of the camp where Esperanza and Mama live and work in California
14. Marta's mother
16. Market owner who is kind to Mexicans
17. Esperanza can feel its heart beating.
20. Summer camp parties held every Sat. night
21. Cause the twins to become ill
22. Author of Esperanza Rising
23. Mexican workers could use it on Friday afternoons

Down

1. Abuelita's sisters who help Mama & Esperanza get their traveling papers
2. What Isabel wants for Christmas
3. Promised Miguel he would help him get a job on the railroad one day
4. Esperanza's maternal grandmother
5. Hortensia's husband; Miguel's father
7. Esperanza cuts these off the potatoes
8. Wants the workers to strike
10. Wants to be the Queen of May
11. Hortensia is from there.
15. Esperanza puts this on her hands to make them soft
17. Wants to marry Mama
18. Papa's last gift to Esperanza
19. Mayor of Aguascalientes
20. Isabel's father

Esperanza Rising Crossword 3 Answer Key

	1		2				3		4		5
	N		A				P	I	N	A	T	A
6 Q	U	I	N	C	E	A	N	E	R	A	
	N			Y		Y			P		B		L
	S			T		E			A		U		F
8 M			H		9 S	10 I	X	T	O		12 F	L	A	N
13 A	R	V	I	N		S			14 A	15 D	A		I		S
R			N			A			X		V		T		O
T			G			B		16 Y	A	K	O	T	A
17 L	A	N	18 D			E			C		C			19 M
U			O			20 J	A	M	A	I	C	A	S
I		21 P	L	U	M	S			U		D			R
S			L			22 R	Y	A	N		O			C
						N				23 P	O	O	L

Across
3. Bought for Mama but given to the campesino family
6. Presentation party for girls at age 15
9. Esperanza's father
12. Made by Josefina to sell at the jamaica
13. Location of the camp where Esperanza and Mama live and work in California
14. Marta's mother
16. Market owner who is kind to Mexicans
17. Esperanza can feel its heart beating.
20. Summer camp parties held every Sat. night
21. Cause the twins to become ill
22. Author of Esperanza Rising
23. Mexican workers could use it on Friday afternoons

Down
1. Abuelita's sisters who help Mama & Esperanza get their traveling papers
2. What Isabel wants for Christmas
3. Promised Miguel he would help him get a job on the railroad one day
4. Esperanza's maternal grandmother
5. Hortensia's husband; Miguel's father
7. Esperanza cuts these off the potatoes
8. Wants the workers to strike
10. Wants to be the Queen of May
11. Hortensia is from there.
15. Esperanza puts this on her hands to make them soft
17. Wants to marry Mama
18. Papa's last gift to Esperanza
19. Mayor of Aguascalientes
20. Isabel's father

Esperanza Rising Crossword 4

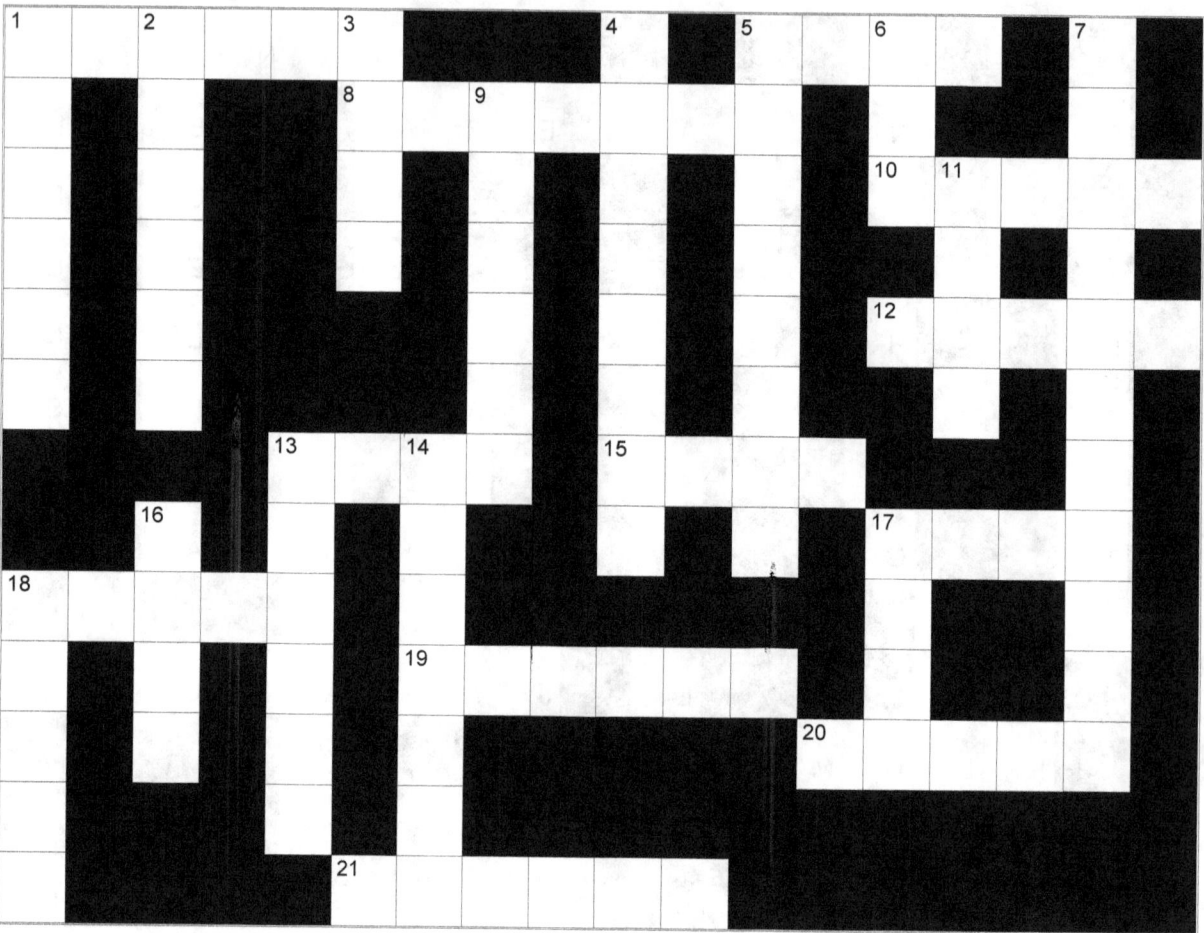

Across
1. Boy Esperanza declared she would marry one day
5. Isabel's father
8. Hortensia's husband; Miguel's father
10. Location of the camp where Esperanza and Mama live and work in California
12. Mayor of Aguascalientes
13. Promised Miguel he would help him get a job on the railroad one day
15. Abuelita's sisters who help Mama & Esperanza get their traveling papers
17. Made by Josefina to sell at the jamaica
18. Makes Esperanza think, 'Bad luck.'
19. Esperanza's mother
20. Miguel's nickname for Esperanza
21. Hortensia is from there.

Down
1. Esperanza's new friend who helps watch the twins
2. Main crop of El Rancho de las Rosas
3. Esperanza can feel its heart beating.
4. What Isabel wants for Christmas
5. Isabel's mother
6. Marta's mother
7. Presentation party for girls at age 15
9. Celebrates the end of harvest & Esperanza's birthday
11. Author of Esperanza Rising
13. Bought for Mama but given to the campesino family
14. Spanish for Head of the Household
16. Papa's last gift to Esperanza
17. Destroys the Ortegas' house
18. Lupe and Pepe

Esperanza Rising Crossword 4 Answer Key

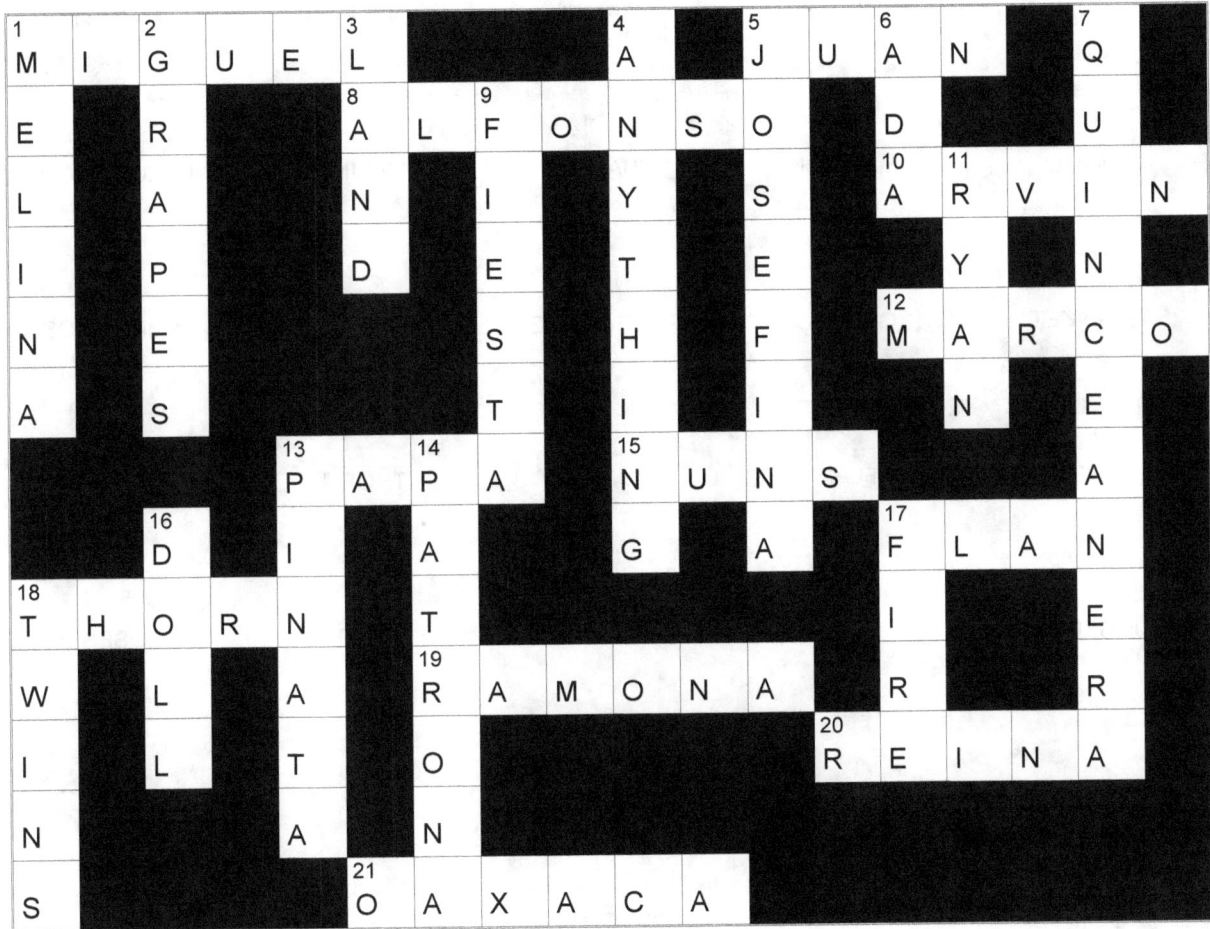

Across
1. Boy Esperanza declared she would marry one day
5. Isabel's father
8. Hortensia's husband; Miguel's father
10. Location of the camp where Esperanza and Mama live and work in California
12. Mayor of Aguascalientes
13. Promised Miguel he would help him get a job on the railroad one day
15. Abuelita's sisters who help Mama & Esperanza get their traveling papers
17. Made by Josefina to sell at the jamaica
18. Makes Esperanza think, 'Bad luck.'
19. Esperanza's mother
20. Miguel's nickname for Esperanza
21. Hortensia is from there.

Down
1. Esperanza's new friend who helps watch the twins
2. Main crop of El Rancho de las Rosas
3. Esperanza can feel its heart beating.
4. What Isabel wants for Christmas
5. Isabel's mother
6. Marta's mother
7. Presentation party for girls at age 15
9. Celebrates the end of harvest & Esperanza's birthday
11. Author of Esperanza Rising
13. Bought for Mama but given to the campesino family
14. Spanish for Head of the Household
16. Papa's last gift to Esperanza
17. Destroys the Ortegas' house
18. Lupe and Pepe

Esperanza Rising

DOLL	SIXTO	CARMEN	HORTENSIA	MARCO
POOL	MARISOL	ISABEL	MELINA	IMMIGRATION
BLANKET	GROTTO	FREE SPACE	FIRE	CAMPESINOS
EYES	FLAN	JAMAICAS	THORN	AGUASCALIENTES
JOSEFINA	LAND	PATRONA	YAKOTA	ROSES

Esperanza Rising

JUAN	PHOENIX	ABUELITA	LUIS	ARVIN
RAILROAD	ALFONSO	FIESTA	GRAPES	ADA
ANYTHING	PINATA	FREE SPACE	MARTA	RAMONA
OAXACA	NUNS	REINA	AVOCADO	SWEEPING
TWINS	MIGUEL	ZIGZAG	RYAN	PAPA

Esperanza Rising

TWINS	MELINA	IMMIGRATION	RAILROAD	ARVIN
CAMPESINOS	PAPA	ADA	PHOENIX	ZIGZAG
PLUMS	RAMONA	FREE SPACE	SWEEPING	FLAN
RYAN	LUIS	CARMEN	AVOCADO	PATRONA
THORN	EYES	HORTENSIA	MIGUEL	MARISOL

Esperanza Rising

JAMAICAS	JOSEFINA	JUAN	AGUASCALIENTES	ABUELITA
ALFONSO	REINA	PINATA	MARCO	ANYTHING
BLANKET	GRAPES	FREE SPACE	ISABEL	FIESTA
YAKOTA	SIXTO	QUINCEANERA	LAND	GROTTO
OAXACA	STRIKERS	FIRE	MARTA	DOLL

Esperanza Rising

PAPA	YAKOTA	JAMAICAS	ROSES	AVOCADO
HORTENSIA	MIGUEL	PATRONA	GRAPES	AGUASCALIENTES
LAND	TWINS	FREE SPACE	CAMPESINOS	ALFONSO
OAXACA	RAMONA	ANYTHING	PHOENIX	MELINA
SIXTO	THORN	MARCO	FLAN	PINATA

Esperanza Rising

SWEEPING	RAILROAD	MARISOL	QUINCEANERA	EYES
NUNS	JUAN	CARMEN	RYAN	ARVIN
DOLL	JOSEFINA	FREE SPACE	REINA	ISABEL
MARTA	GROTTO	FIESTA	FIRE	ZIGZAG
BLANKET	ABUELITA	STRIKERS	LUIS	ADA

Esperanza Rising

CAMPESINOS	REINA	ROSES	RAMONA	JUAN
ANYTHING	SIXTO	QUINCEANERA	EYES	DOLL
TWINS	JOSEFINA	FREE SPACE	RAILROAD	AVOCADO
ADA	MARISOL	ALFONSO	HORTENSIA	ZIGZAG
MELINA	PHOENIX	BLANKET	PATRONA	ARVIN

Esperanza Rising

MIGUEL	STRIKERS	PINATA	POOL	IMMIGRATION
OAXACA	LUIS	GRAPES	SWEEPING	MARCO
ISABEL	PLUMS	FREE SPACE	YAKOTA	ABUELITA
JAMAICAS	RYAN	PAPA	FIESTA	FLAN
LAND	AGUASCALIENTES	GROTTO	THORN	NUNS

Esperanza Rising

TWINS	MARTA	THORN	JAMAICAS	ALFONSO
FLAN	YAKOTA	SIXTO	ZIGZAG	ROSES
SWEEPING	ARVIN	FREE SPACE	MELINA	IMMIGRATION
PAPA	RAMONA	ADA	CAMPESINOS	GROTTO
GRAPES	STRIKERS	ISABEL	DOLL	REINA

Esperanza Rising

NUNS	RYAN	LUIS	AGUASCALIENTES	PATRONA
AVOCADO	LAND	QUINCEANERA	JOSEFINA	FIESTA
EYES	MARCO	FREE SPACE	CARMEN	PLUMS
PINATA	JUAN	ABUELITA	MARISOL	OAXACA
MIGUEL	FIRE	RAILROAD	HORTENSIA	BLANKET

Esperanza Rising

FIRE	GRAPES	RAILROAD	DOLL	MARTA
EYES	THORN	SIXTO	JUAN	HORTENSIA
BLANKET	FIESTA	FREE SPACE	YAKOTA	JOSEFINA
MELINA	FLAN	ARVIN	STRIKERS	ISABEL
ABUELITA	PATRONA	PLUMS	AVOCADO	ZIGZAG

Esperanza Rising

JAMAICAS	TWINS	RAMONA	CARMEN	REINA
PHOENIX	QUINCEANERA	LAND	ANYTHING	AGUASCALIENTES
OAXACA	RYAN	FREE SPACE	ROSES	MARISOL
PINATA	PAPA	POOL	GROTTO	MARCO
CAMPESINOS	LUIS	NUNS	ADA	IMMIGRATION

Esperanza Rising

PINATA	SIXTO	ZIGZAG	PATRONA	LUIS
FIESTA	YAKOTA	ALFONSO	AGUASCALIENTES	TWINS
ANYTHING	MARCO	FREE SPACE	ROSES	CARMEN
EYES	ISABEL	BLANKET	ADA	ARVIN
FLAN	GRAPES	HORTENSIA	OAXACA	AVOCADO

Esperanza Rising

POOL	JOSEFINA	MIGUEL	ABUELITA	FIRE
JUAN	MELINA	MARISOL	GROTTO	STRIKERS
MARTA	REINA	FREE SPACE	NUNS	IMMIGRATION
DOLL	SWEEPING	PAPA	PHOENIX	RAILROAD
JAMAICAS	THORN	RYAN	CAMPESINOS	RAMONA

Esperanza Rising

MELINA	JOSEFINA	RAILROAD	MARCO	EYES
ROSES	ZIGZAG	JUAN	SIXTO	AGUASCALIENTES
QUINCEANERA	AVOCADO	FREE SPACE	JAMAICAS	BLANKET
ANYTHING	GRAPES	ABUELITA	THORN	YAKOTA
PHOENIX	PAPA	PINATA	MIGUEL	CARMEN

Esperanza Rising

FLAN	ALFONSO	RAMONA	HORTENSIA	GROTTO
PATRONA	ARVIN	ADA	STRIKERS	ISABEL
OAXACA	REINA	FREE SPACE	FIRE	CAMPESINOS
PLUMS	NUNS	POOL	RYAN	FIESTA
MARTA	TWINS	IMMIGRATION	SWEEPING	LUIS

Esperanza Rising

LUIS	ZIGZAG	JOSEFINA	ANYTHING	PINATA
RAMONA	LAND	DOLL	RAILROAD	RYAN
QUINCEANERA	STRIKERS	FREE SPACE	POOL	GROTTO
CARMEN	SIXTO	GRAPES	MELINA	ADA
ARVIN	CAMPESINOS	THORN	MARTA	IMMIGRATION

Esperanza Rising

SWEEPING	EYES	MIGUEL	PATRONA	REINA
FLAN	ABUELITA	ALFONSO	TWINS	YAKOTA
NUNS	JAMAICAS	FREE SPACE	FIESTA	HORTENSIA
PLUMS	AVOCADO	AGUASCALIENTES	BLANKET	MARISOL
OAXACA	JUAN	MARCO	PAPA	PHOENIX

Esperanza Rising

OAXACA	ANYTHING	AVOCADO	ROSES	JOSEFINA
NUNS	HORTENSIA	ISABEL	ABUELITA	CAMPESINOS
QUINCEANERA	REINA	FREE SPACE	YAKOTA	SIXTO
FIESTA	PINATA	ADA	SWEEPING	JUAN
ZIGZAG	FLAN	FIRE	LAND	PATRONA

Esperanza Rising

TWINS	PLUMS	LUIS	BLANKET	ALFONSO
JAMAICAS	IMMIGRATION	AGUASCALIENTES	THORN	PHOENIX
DOLL	EYES	FREE SPACE	MIGUEL	POOL
STRIKERS	MARTA	RAMONA	ARVIN	RYAN
CARMEN	MARCO	RAILROAD	GROTTO	PAPA

Esperanza Rising

FIRE	CARMEN	ABUELITA	ADA	RYAN
RAMONA	MIGUEL	LUIS	SIXTO	PAPA
MELINA	LAND	FREE SPACE	QUINCEANERA	ZIGZAG
ISABEL	IMMIGRATION	PLUMS	DOLL	GROTTO
PINATA	MARISOL	RAILROAD	FIESTA	GRAPES

Esperanza Rising

THORN	EYES	MARCO	ROSES	CAMPESINOS
AGUASCALIENTES	BLANKET	FLAN	JAMAICAS	JOSEFINA
AVOCADO	SWEEPING	FREE SPACE	ANYTHING	POOL
OAXACA	HORTENSIA	PATRONA	ARVIN	NUNS
TWINS	ALFONSO	STRIKERS	JUAN	REINA

Esperanza Rising

RYAN	GRAPES	IMMIGRATION	HORTENSIA	FIESTA
FLAN	JAMAICAS	ARVIN	DOLL	TWINS
AGUASCALIENTES	JUAN	FREE SPACE	ANYTHING	POOL
PLUMS	MARTA	ADA	ROSES	CAMPESINOS
SWEEPING	YAKOTA	AVOCADO	MELINA	PAPA

Esperanza Rising

MARCO	QUINCEANERA	RAILROAD	NUNS	PATRONA
GROTTO	LAND	OAXACA	THORN	ISABEL
PHOENIX	STRIKERS	FREE SPACE	ALFONSO	SIXTO
ABUELITA	REINA	MIGUEL	LUIS	JOSEFINA
ZIGZAG	MARISOL	PINATA	FIRE	EYES

Esperanza Rising

ALFONSO	ARVIN	SIXTO	ABUELITA	JUAN
POOL	FIRE	NUNS	EYES	GRAPES
IMMIGRATION	LUIS	FREE SPACE	THORN	FIESTA
ROSES	SWEEPING	TWINS	MIGUEL	DOLL
OAXACA	AVOCADO	RAMONA	ISABEL	PLUMS

Esperanza Rising

JAMAICAS	AGUASCALIENTES	ZIGZAG	PATRONA	STRIKERS
QUINCEANERA	MARISOL	PHOENIX	PINATA	MARCO
PAPA	YAKOTA	FREE SPACE	ANYTHING	GROTTO
MELINA	CARMEN	HORTENSIA	ADA	FLAN
LAND	BLANKET	RAILROAD	RYAN	MARTA

Esperanza Rising

MARTA	JUAN	SIXTO	ABUELITA	ADA
JAMAICAS	REINA	FIRE	IMMIGRATION	FLAN
DOLL	RAILROAD	FREE SPACE	ZIGZAG	PHOENIX
LUIS	PATRONA	PINATA	FIESTA	LAND
ANYTHING	ROSES	GRAPES	ALFONSO	NUNS

Esperanza Rising

THORN	ARVIN	RAMONA	CAMPESINOS	TWINS
MARCO	ISABEL	AVOCADO	AGUASCALIENTES	QUINCEANERA
PLUMS	RYAN	FREE SPACE	PAPA	HORTENSIA
CARMEN	MIGUEL	OAXACA	EYES	STRIKERS
YAKOTA	MELINA	SWEEPING	BLANKET	GROTTO

Esperanza Rising

JOSEFINA	GROTTO	PHOENIX	DOLL	MIGUEL
PAPA	ABUELITA	ALFONSO	QUINCEANERA	EYES
SWEEPING	NUNS	FREE SPACE	THORN	TWINS
CARMEN	CAMPESINOS	MARTA	OAXACA	ANYTHING
HORTENSIA	YAKOTA	AGUASCALIENTES	ROSES	PATRONA

Esperanza Rising

RAMONA	ADA	MARISOL	STRIKERS	PINATA
JUAN	ISABEL	MELINA	JAMAICAS	FLAN
ARVIN	REINA	FREE SPACE	RYAN	RAILROAD
BLANKET	AVOCADO	LUIS	FIRE	LAND
MARCO	IMMIGRATION	PLUMS	SIXTO	GRAPES

Esperanza Rising

ABUELITA	GROTTO	JAMAICAS	SIXTO	PATRONA
IMMIGRATION	FLAN	TWINS	PHOENIX	ISABEL
FIRE	HORTENSIA	FREE SPACE	BLANKET	PINATA
JOSEFINA	EYES	RYAN	RAILROAD	QUINCEANERA
SWEEPING	YAKOTA	ANYTHING	ADA	ROSES

Esperanza Rising

FIESTA	AGUASCALIENTES	RAMONA	CARMEN	ALFONSO
MARISOL	CAMPESINOS	AVOCADO	JUAN	STRIKERS
REINA	OAXACA	FREE SPACE	GRAPES	LUIS
MELINA	MARTA	THORN	POOL	MIGUEL
PAPA	LAND	PLUMS	NUNS	ZIGZAG

Esperanza Rising Vocabulary Word List

No.	Word	Clue/Definition
1.	ACCOSTING	Approaching boldly or aggressively
2.	ACCUSTOMED	Being in the habit of
3.	AMBUSHED	Attacked from a hidden position
4.	ANTICIPATED	Looked forward to; expected
5.	BEREFT	Without; lacking
6.	BESTOWED	Presented as a gift; given
7.	BROODED	Was in a state of gloomy, serious thought
8.	BUOYED	Heartened or inspired; uplifted
9.	CAPRICIOUS	Tending to change abruptly without apparent reason
10.	CAREENING	Wobbling or swerving while in motion, usually at high speed
11.	CASCADE	Rush down in large amounts
12.	CONDOLENCES	Expressions of sympathy for a person who is suffering sorrow, misfortune or grief
13.	COPE	Face and deal with responsibilities, problems, or difficulties
14.	CORDIAL	Friendly; warm
15.	CORRUPT	Guilty of dishonest practices; untrustworthy
16.	COT	Light, portable bed, esp. one of canvas on a folding frame
17.	DEBRIS	Remains of anything broken down or destroyed; ruins; rubble
18.	DEMEANOR	Conduct; behavior; manner
19.	DEPORTATIONS	Lawful removal of illegal immigrants
20.	DESPONDENT	Depressed; gloomy
21.	DEVOUTLY	Expressing devotion or faith
22.	DOTING	Being excessively fond of
23.	DROWSY	Sleepy
24.	DWINDLED	Made smaller or less
25.	ERUPTED	Emerged violently
26.	ESCORTED	Went along with to protect or aid
27.	EXTRAVAGANT	Tending towards extreme or excessive spending
28.	FORLORN	Lonely and sad; unhappy and neglected
29.	FRANTICALLY	Characterized by rapid and disordered or nervous activity
30.	FRAYED	Worn away or tattered along the edges
31.	GINGERLY	With great care or caution
32.	IMMUNIZED	Protected from a disease
33.	INDEBTED	Owing for favors or kindness received
34.	INFURIATED	Very angry
35.	INTENT	Sharply focused on something
36.	JALOPY	Falling-apart automobile
37.	MAKESHIFT	Made from whatever materials are available rather than usual means
38.	MARVELED	Looked at with wonder, admiration, or shock
39.	MENACING	Threatening to cause evil, harm, or injury
40.	MESMERIZED	Spellbound; fascinated
41.	MONOTONOUS	Lacking in variety; boring
42.	MUSSED	Messy or untidy; rumpled
43.	OPTIMISM	Characteristic in which someone looks on the positive side of things
44.	PENETRATE	Pierce or pass into or through
45.	PERSISTENT	Determined; refusing to give up
46.	PLAITED	Braided
47.	PREOCCUPIED	Completely lost in thought
48.	PUNGENT	Sour or biting in smell or taste

Esperanza Rising Vocabulary Word List

No. Word	Clue/Definition
49. RECLINING	Leaning back
50. REGAL	Grand; fit for royalty
51. RELAPSE	Return of a disease or illness after partial recovery from it
52. RELUCTANTLY	Unwillingly; disinclined
53. RENEGADES	Outlaws; rebels
54. RESENTMENT	Feeling of displeasure from a sense of being injured or offended
55. RESOUNDING	Making an echoing sound
56. RETRIEVED	Recovered or regained
57. RIVETED	Fastened (the eye, attention, etc.) firmly to something
58. SALVAGE	Saving something from fire, danger, etc.
59. SCORN	Treat or regard with disrespect or shame
60. SCYTHE	Tool with a long, single-edged blade set at an angle for cutting grass or grain
61. SERENADED	Entertained with a musical performance, esp. by a lover under the window of his sweetheart
62. SHRINE	Structure or place blessed or devoted to some holy person
63. SKEINS	Lengths of thread or yarn wound in a loose coil
64. SOLEMNLY	Seriously
65. SPEWING	Shooting out forcefully, usually in an uncontrolled manner
66. SQUALOR	Condition of filth and misery
67. STAGNANT	Not flowing or running, as water, air, etc.
68. STRIKE	Refuse to do work because of a disagreement with an employer over pay or conditions
69. SUPPLENESS	Flexibility
70. SUSCEPTIBLE	Easily influenced; weak
71. TALLOW	Solid fat taken from animals used for making candles, soaps, etc.
72. TAUNTING	Teasing
73. TAUT	Tightly drawn; tense
74. TORMENTED	Experiencing intense pain, especially mental pain
75. TORRENT	Stream of water flowing with great speed, force & violence
76. UNDULATING	Having a wave-like or rippled form or surface
77. VALISE	Small piece of luggage
78. VAPORS	Visible breath, as fog, mist, steam, smoke, or gas
79. VENOM	Poison
80. WEARY	Tired
81. WILTED	Limp; drooped; sagging or falling over
82. YEARNING	Unsatisfied desire

Esperanza Rising Vocabulary Fill In The Blanks 1

_____

_____

_____

_____

_____

_____

_____

_____

_____

_____

_____

_____

_____

_____

_____

_____

_____

_____

_____

_____

1. Lengths of thread or yarn wound in a loose coil
2. Lacking in variety; boring
3. Unwillingly; disinclined
4. Solid fat taken from animals used for making candles, soaps, etc.
5. Tending to change abruptly without apparent reason
6. Tired
7. Worn away or tattered along the edges
8. Expressions of sympathy for a person who is suffering sorrow, misfortune or grief
9. Lawful removal of illegal immigrants
10. Remains of anything broken down or destroyed; ruins; rubble
11. Falling-apart automobile
12. Flexibility
13. Pierce or pass into or through
14. Making an echoing sound
15. Depressed; gloomy
16. Poison
17. Messy or untidy; rumpled
18. Experiencing intense pain, especially mental pain
19. Braided
20. Visible breath, as fog, mist, steam, smoke, or gas

Esperanza Rising Vocabulary Fill In The Blanks 1 Answer Key

SKEINS	1. Lengths of thread or yarn wound in a loose coil
MONOTONOUS	2. Lacking in variety; boring
RELUCTANTLY	3. Unwillingly; disinclined
TALLOW	4. Solid fat taken from animals used for making candles, soaps, etc.
CAPRICIOUS	5. Tending to change abruptly without apparent reason
WEARY	6. Tired
FRAYED	7. Worn away or tattered along the edges
CONDOLENCES	8. Expressions of sympathy for a person who is suffering sorrow, misfortune or grief
DEPORTATIONS	9. Lawful removal of illegal immigrants
DEBRIS	10. Remains of anything broken down or destroyed; ruins; rubble
JALOPY	11. Falling-apart automobile
SUPPLENESS	12. Flexibility
PENETRATE	13. Pierce or pass into or through
RESOUNDING	14. Making an echoing sound
DESPONDENT	15. Depressed; gloomy
VENOM	16. Poison
MUSSED	17. Messy or untidy; rumpled
TORMENTED	18. Experiencing intense pain, especially mental pain
PLAITED	19. Braided
VAPORS	20. Visible breath, as fog, mist, steam, smoke, or gas

Esperanza Rising Vocabulary Fill In The Blanks 2

_____

1. Very angry
2. Stream of water flowing with great speed, force & violence
3. Experiencing intense pain, especially mental pain
4. Light, portable bed, esp. one of canvas on a folding frame
5. Flexibility
6. Without; lacking
7. Protected from a disease
8. Saving something from fire, danger, etc.
9. Lawful removal of illegal immigrants
10. Entertained with a musical performance, esp. by a lover under the window of his sweetheart
11. Characterized by rapid and disordered or nervous activity
12. Feeling of displeasure from a sense of being injured or offended
13. Making an echoing sound
14. Tool with a long, single-edged blade set at an angle for cutting grass or grain
15. Rush down in large amounts
16. Visible breath, as fog, mist, steam, smoke, or gas
17. Unsatisfied desire
18. Solid fat taken from animals used for making candles, soaps, etc.
19. Characteristic in which someone looks on the positive side of things
20. Tightly drawn; tense

Esperanza Rising Vocabulary Fill In The Blanks 2 Answer Key

INFURIATED	1. Very angry
TORRENT	2. Stream of water flowing with great speed, force & violence
TORMENTED	3. Experiencing intense pain, especially mental pain
COT	4. Light, portable bed, esp. one of canvas on a folding frame
SUPPLENESS	5. Flexibility
BEREFT	6. Without; lacking
IMMUNIZED	7. Protected from a disease
SALVAGE	8. Saving something from fire, danger, etc.
DEPORTATIONS	9. Lawful removal of illegal immigrants
SERENADED	10. Entertained with a musical performance, esp. by a lover under the window of his sweetheart
FRANTICALLY	11. Characterized by rapid and disordered or nervous activity
RESENTMENT	12. Feeling of displeasure from a sense of being injured or offended
RESOUNDING	13. Making an echoing sound
SCYTHE	14. Tool with a long, single-edged blade set at an angle for cutting grass or grain
CASCADE	15. Rush down in large amounts
VAPORS	16. Visible breath, as fog, mist, steam, smoke, or gas
YEARNING	17. Unsatisfied desire
TALLOW	18. Solid fat taken from animals used for making candles, soaps, etc.
OPTIMISM	19. Characteristic in which someone looks on the positive side of things
TAUT	20. Tightly drawn; tense

Esperanza Rising Vocabulary Fill In The Blanks 3

1. Saving something from fire, danger, etc.
2. Pierce or pass into or through
3. Making an echoing sound
4. Spellbound; fascinated
5. Having a wave-like or rippled form or surface
6. Structure or place blessed or devoted to some holy person
7. Sour or biting in smell or taste
8. Looked at with wonder, admiration, or shock
9. Seriously
10. Characteristic in which someone looks on the positive side of things
11. Teasing
12. Remains of anything broken down or destroyed; ruins; rubble
13. Lawful removal of illegal immigrants
14. Lengths of thread or yarn wound in a loose coil
15. Sleepy
16. Completely lost in thought
17. Expressing devotion or faith
18. Guilty of dishonest practices; untrustworthy
19. Stream of water flowing with great speed, force & violence
20. Approaching boldly or aggressively

Esperanza Rising Vocabulary Fill In The Blanks 3 Answer Key

SALVAGE	1. Saving something from fire, danger, etc.
PENETRATE	2. Pierce or pass into or through
RESOUNDING	3. Making an echoing sound
MESMERIZED	4. Spellbound; fascinated
UNDULATING	5. Having a wave-like or rippled form or surface
SHRINE	6. Structure or place blessed or devoted to some holy person
PUNGENT	7. Sour or biting in smell or taste
MARVELED	8. Looked at with wonder, admiration, or shock
SOLEMNLY	9. Seriously
OPTIMISM	10. Characteristic in which someone looks on the positive side of things
TAUNTING	11. Teasing
DEBRIS	12. Remains of anything broken down or destroyed; ruins; rubble
DEPORTATIONS	13. Lawful removal of illegal immigrants
SKEINS	14. Lengths of thread or yarn wound in a loose coil
DROWSY	15. Sleepy
PREOCCUPIED	16. Completely lost in thought
DEVOUTLY	17. Expressing devotion or faith
CORRUPT	18. Guilty of dishonest practices; untrustworthy
TORRENT	19. Stream of water flowing with great speed, force & violence
ACCOSTING	20. Approaching boldly or aggressively

Esperanza Rising Vocabulary Fill In The Blanks 4

1. Treat or regard with disrespect or shame
2. Tending to change abruptly without apparent reason
3. Having a wave-like or rippled form or surface
4. Emerged violently
5. Saving something from fire, danger, etc.
6. Rush down in large amounts
7. Small piece of luggage
8. Leaning back
9. Owing for favors or kindness received
10. Completely lost in thought
11. Grand; fit for royalty
12. Spellbound; fascinated
13. Tired
14. Flexibility
15. Visible breath, as fog, mist, steam, smoke, or gas
16. Easily influenced; weak
17. Limp; drooped; sagging or falling over
18. Solid fat taken from animals used for making candles, soaps, etc.
19. Unsatisfied desire
20. Stream of water flowing with great speed, force & violence

Esperanza Rising Vocabulary Fill In The Blanks 4 Answer Key

SCORN	1. Treat or regard with disrespect or shame
CAPRICIOUS	2. Tending to change abruptly without apparent reason
UNDULATING	3. Having a wave-like or rippled form or surface
ERUPTED	4. Emerged violently
SALVAGE	5. Saving something from fire, danger, etc.
CASCADE	6. Rush down in large amounts
VALISE	7. Small piece of luggage
RECLINING	8. Leaning back
INDEBTED	9. Owing for favors or kindness received
PREOCCUPIED	10. Completely lost in thought
REGAL	11. Grand; fit for royalty
MESMERIZED	12. Spellbound; fascinated
WEARY	13. Tired
SUPPLENESS	14. Flexibility
VAPORS	15. Visible breath, as fog, mist, steam, smoke, or gas
SUSCEPTIBLE	16. Easily influenced; weak
WILTED	17. Limp; drooped; sagging or falling over
TALLOW	18. Solid fat taken from animals used for making candles, soaps, etc.
YEARNING	19. Unsatisfied desire
TORRENT	20. Stream of water flowing with great speed, force & violence

Esperanza Rising Vocabulary Matching 1

___ 1. RELUCTANTLY	A. Outlaws; rebels
___ 2. WEARY	B. Falling-apart automobile
___ 3. DESPONDENT	C. Feeling of displeasure from a sense of being injured or offended
___ 4. MARVELED	D. Protected from a disease
___ 5. VALISE	E. Looked at with wonder, admiration, or shock
___ 6. RENEGADES	F. Sour or biting in smell or taste
___ 7. JALOPY	G. Depressed; gloomy
___ 8. MONOTONOUS	H. Lacking in variety; boring
___ 9. IMMUNIZED	I. Not flowing or running, as water, air, etc.
___10. FRANTICALLY	J. Unwillingly; disinclined
___11. PENETRATE	K. Wobbling or swerving while in motion, usually at high speed
___12. SKEINS	L. Entertained with a musical performance, esp. by a lover under the window of his sweetheart
___13. TORRENT	M. Worn away or tattered along the edges
___14. PUNGENT	N. Recovered or regained
___15. STAGNANT	O. Pierce or pass into or through
___16. CASCADE	P. Structure or place blessed or devoted to some holy person
___17. DEMEANOR	Q. Characterized by rapid and disordered or nervous activity
___18. INDEBTED	R. Conduct; behavior; manner
___19. RETRIEVED	S. Lengths of thread or yarn wound in a loose coil
___20. RESENTMENT	T. Stream of water flowing with great speed, force & violence
___21. SHRINE	U. Tired
___22. FRAYED	V. Small piece of luggage
___23. SERENADED	W. Rush down in large amounts
___24. CAREENING	X. Heartened or inspired; uplifted
___25. BUOYED	Y. Owing for favors or kindness received

Esperanza Rising Vocabulary Matching 1 Answer Key

J - 1. RELUCTANTLY
U - 2. WEARY
G - 3. DESPONDENT
E - 4. MARVELED
V - 5. VALISE
A - 6. RENEGADES
B - 7. JALOPY
H - 8. MONOTONOUS
D - 9. IMMUNIZED
Q - 10. FRANTICALLY
O - 11. PENETRATE
S - 12. SKEINS
T - 13. TORRENT
F - 14. PUNGENT
I - 15. STAGNANT
W - 16. CASCADE
R - 17. DEMEANOR
Y - 18. INDEBTED
N - 19. RETRIEVED
C - 20. RESENTMENT
P - 21. SHRINE
M - 22. FRAYED
L - 23. SERENADED
K - 24. CAREENING
X - 25. BUOYED

A. Outlaws; rebels
B. Falling-apart automobile
C. Feeling of displeasure from a sense of being injured or offended
D. Protected from a disease
E. Looked at with wonder, admiration, or shock
F. Sour or biting in smell or taste
G. Depressed; gloomy
H. Lacking in variety; boring
I. Not flowing or running, as water, air, etc.
J. Unwillingly; disinclined
K. Wobbling or swerving while in motion, usually at high speed
L. Entertained with a musical performance, esp. by a lover under the window of his sweetheart
M. Worn away or tattered along the edges
N. Recovered or regained
O. Pierce or pass into or through
P. Structure or place blessed or devoted to some holy person
Q. Characterized by rapid and disordered or nervous activity
R. Conduct; behavior; manner
S. Lengths of thread or yarn wound in a loose coil
T. Stream of water flowing with great speed, force & violence
U. Tired
V. Small piece of luggage
W. Rush down in large amounts
X. Heartened or inspired; uplifted
Y. Owing for favors or kindness received

Esperanza Rising Vocabulary Matching 2

___ 1. DEMEANOR
___ 2. PREOCCUPIED
___ 3. ESCORTED
___ 4. DWINDLED
___ 5. DROWSY
___ 6. ERUPTED
___ 7. PERSISTENT
___ 8. CAREENING
___ 9. DOTING
___ 10. INTENT
___ 11. TAUNTING
___ 12. MARVELED
___ 13. STRIKE
___ 14. SUSCEPTIBLE
___ 15. OPTIMISM
___ 16. INDEBTED
___ 17. WILTED
___ 18. DEVOUTLY
___ 19. MONOTONOUS
___ 20. REGAL
___ 21. DEPORTATIONS
___ 22. ANTICIPATED
___ 23. TORRENT
___ 24. SOLEMNLY
___ 25. DEBRIS

A. Wobbling or swerving while in motion, usually at high speed
B. Sleepy
C. Completely lost in thought
D. Made smaller or less
E. Stream of water flowing with great speed, force & violence
F. Determined; refusing to give up
G. Limp; drooped; sagging or falling over
H. Seriously
I. Easily influenced; weak
J. Emerged violently
K. Lacking in variety; boring
L. Characteristic in which someone looks on the positive side of things
M. Remains of anything broken down or destroyed; ruins; rubble
N. Went along with to protect or aid
O. Teasing
P. Owing for favors or kindness received
Q. Refuse to do work because of a disagreement with an employer over pay or conditions
R. Expressing devotion or faith
S. Being excessively fond of
T. Looked at with wonder, admiration, or shock
U. Looked forward to; expected
V. Lawful removal of illegal immigrants
W. Grand; fit for royalty
X. Sharply focused on something
Y. Conduct; behavior; manner

Esperanza Rising Vocabulary Matching 2 Answer Key

Y - 1. DEMEANOR		A. Wobbling or swerving while in motion, usually at high speed
C - 2. PREOCCUPIED		B. Sleepy
N - 3. ESCORTED		C. Completely lost in thought
D - 4. DWINDLED		D. Made smaller or less
B - 5. DROWSY		E. Stream of water flowing with great speed, force & violence
J - 6. ERUPTED		F. Determined; refusing to give up
F - 7. PERSISTENT		G. Limp; drooped; sagging or falling over
A - 8. CAREENING		H. Seriously
S - 9. DOTING		I. Easily influenced; weak
X - 10. INTENT		J. Emerged violently
O - 11. TAUNTING		K. Lacking in variety; boring
T - 12. MARVELED		L. Characteristic in which someone looks on the positive side of things
Q - 13. STRIKE		M. Remains of anything broken down or destroyed; ruins; rubble
I - 14. SUSCEPTIBLE		N. Went along with to protect or aid
L - 15. OPTIMISM		O. Teasing
P - 16. INDEBTED		P. Owing for favors or kindness received
G - 17. WILTED		Q. Refuse to do work because of a disagreement with an employer over pay or conditions
R - 18. DEVOUTLY		R. Expressing devotion or faith
K - 19. MONOTONOUS		S. Being excessively fond of
W - 20. REGAL		T. Looked at with wonder, admiration, or shock
V - 21. DEPORTATIONS		U. Looked forward to; expected
U - 22. ANTICIPATED		V. Lawful removal of illegal immigrants
E - 23. TORRENT		W. Grand; fit for royalty
H - 24. SOLEMNLY		X. Sharply focused on something
M - 25. DEBRIS		Y. Conduct; behavior; manner

Esperanza Rising Vocabulary Matching 3

___ 1. SERENADED
___ 2. ACCUSTOMED
___ 3. CORDIAL
___ 4. MESMERIZED
___ 5. SHRINE
___ 6. FORLORN
___ 7. TORMENTED
___ 8. RENEGADES
___ 9. TAUNTING
___ 10. RIVETED
___ 11. DEBRIS
___ 12. DEPORTATIONS
___ 13. SOLEMNLY
___ 14. SKEINS
___ 15. YEARNING
___ 16. BROODED
___ 17. DOTING
___ 18. MONOTONOUS
___ 19. SALVAGE
___ 20. PLAITED
___ 21. SUPPLENESS
___ 22. ANTICIPATED
___ 23. STAGNANT
___ 24. CAREENING
___ 25. INDEBTED

A. Looked forward to; expected
B. Remains of anything broken down or destroyed; ruins; rubble
C. Lacking in variety; boring
D. Experiencing intense pain, especially mental pain
E. Fastened (the eye, attention, etc.) firmly to something
F. Friendly; warm
G. Wobbling or swerving while in motion, usually at high speed
H. Unsatisfied desire
I. Was in a state of gloomy, serious thought
J. Not flowing or running, as water, air, etc.
K. Braided
L. Flexibility
M. Structure or place blessed or devoted to some holy person
N. Being in the habit of
O. Saving something from fire, danger, etc.
P. Teasing
Q. Lengths of thread or yarn wound in a loose coil
R. Lonely and sad; unhappy and neglected
S. Being excessively fond of
T. Owing for favors or kindness received
U. Spellbound; fascinated
V. Seriously
W. Lawful removal of illegal immigrants
X. Entertained with a musical performance, esp. by a lover under the window of his sweetheart
Y. Outlaws; rebels

Esperanza Rising Vocabulary Matching 3 Answer Key

X - 1. SERENADED
N - 2. ACCUSTOMED
F - 3. CORDIAL
U - 4. MESMERIZED
M - 5. SHRINE
R - 6. FORLORN
D - 7. TORMENTED
Y - 8. RENEGADES
P - 9. TAUNTING
E - 10. RIVETED
B - 11. DEBRIS
W - 12. DEPORTATIONS
V - 13. SOLEMNLY
Q - 14. SKEINS
H - 15. YEARNING
I - 16. BROODED
S - 17. DOTING
C - 18. MONOTONOUS
O - 19. SALVAGE
K - 20. PLAITED
L - 21. SUPPLENESS
A - 22. ANTICIPATED
J - 23. STAGNANT
G - 24. CAREENING
T - 25. INDEBTED

A. Looked forward to; expected
B. Remains of anything broken down or destroyed; ruins; rubble
C. Lacking in variety; boring
D. Experiencing intense pain, especially mental pain
E. Fastened (the eye, attention, etc.) firmly to something
F. Friendly; warm
G. Wobbling or swerving while in motion, usually at high speed
H. Unsatisfied desire
I. Was in a state of gloomy, serious thought
J. Not flowing or running, as water, air, etc.
K. Braided
L. Flexibility
M. Structure or place blessed or devoted to some holy person
N. Being in the habit of
O. Saving something from fire, danger, etc.
P. Teasing
Q. Lengths of thread or yarn wound in a loose coil
R. Lonely and sad; unhappy and neglected
S. Being excessively fond of
T. Owing for favors or kindness received
U. Spellbound; fascinated
V. Seriously
W. Lawful removal of illegal immigrants
X. Entertained with a musical performance, esp. by a lover under the window of his sweetheart
Y. Outlaws; rebels

Esperanza Rising Vocabulary Matching 4

___ 1. PLAITED
___ 2. ESCORTED
___ 3. TORRENT
___ 4. COPE
___ 5. VAPORS
___ 6. MENACING
___ 7. SQUALOR
___ 8. WILTED
___ 9. UNDULATING
___ 10. CAREENING
___ 11. CONDOLENCES
___ 12. DWINDLED
___ 13. DOTING
___ 14. SUSCEPTIBLE
___ 15. TALLOW
___ 16. SPEWING
___ 17. SCORN
___ 18. BUOYED
___ 19. DEMEANOR
___ 20. MONOTONOUS
___ 21. INTENT
___ 22. OPTIMISM
___ 23. PERSISTENT
___ 24. CAPRICIOUS
___ 25. CORRUPT

A. Stream of water flowing with great speed, force & violence
B. Limp; drooped; sagging or falling over
C. Conduct; behavior; manner
D. Shooting out forcefully, usually in an uncontrolled manner
E. Determined; refusing to give up
F. Tending to change abruptly without apparent reason
G. Treat or regard with disrespect or shame
H. Braided
I. Expressions of sympathy for a person who is suffering sorrow, misfortune or grief
J. Having a wave-like or rippled form or surface
K. Condition of filth and misery
L. Characteristic in which someone looks on the positive side of things
M. Threatening to cause evil, harm, or injury
N. Easily influenced; weak
O. Made smaller or less
P. Guilty of dishonest practices; untrustworthy
Q. Heartened or inspired; uplifted
R. Visible breath, as fog, mist, steam, smoke, or gas
S. Being excessively fond of
T. Wobbling or swerving while in motion, usually at high speed
U. Solid fat taken from animals used for making candles, soaps, etc.
V. Went along with to protect or aid
W. Sharply focused on something
X. Lacking in variety; boring
Y. Face and deal with responsibilities, problems, or difficulties

Esperanza Rising Vocabulary Matching 4 Answer Key

H - 1. PLAITED
V - 2. ESCORTED
A - 3. TORRENT
Y - 4. COPE
R - 5. VAPORS
M - 6. MENACING
K - 7. SQUALOR
B - 8. WILTED
J - 9. UNDULATING
T - 10. CAREENING
I - 11. CONDOLENCES
O - 12. DWINDLED
S - 13. DOTING
N - 14. SUSCEPTIBLE
U - 15. TALLOW
D - 16. SPEWING
G - 17. SCORN
Q - 18. BUOYED
C - 19. DEMEANOR
X - 20. MONOTONOUS
W - 21. INTENT
L - 22. OPTIMISM
E - 23. PERSISTENT
F - 24. CAPRICIOUS
P - 25. CORRUPT

A. Stream of water flowing with great speed, force & violence
B. Limp; drooped; sagging or falling over
C. Conduct; behavior; manner
D. Shooting out forcefully, usually in an uncontrolled manner
E. Determined; refusing to give up
F. Tending to change abruptly without apparent reason
G. Treat or regard with disrespect or shame
H. Braided
I. Expressions of sympathy for a person who is suffering sorrow, misfortune or grief
J. Having a wave-like or rippled form or surface
K. Condition of filth and misery
L. Characteristic in which someone looks on the positive side of things
M. Threatening to cause evil, harm, or injury
N. Easily influenced; weak
O. Made smaller or less
P. Guilty of dishonest practices; untrustworthy
Q. Heartened or inspired; uplifted
R. Visible breath, as fog, mist, steam, smoke, or gas
S. Being excessively fond of
T. Wobbling or swerving while in motion, usually at high speed
U. Solid fat taken from animals used for making candles, soaps, etc.
V. Went along with to protect or aid
W. Sharply focused on something
X. Lacking in variety; boring
Y. Face and deal with responsibilities, problems, or difficulties

Esperanza Rising Vocabulary Magic Squares 1

Match the definition with the vocabulary word. Put your answers in the magic squares below. When your answers are correct, all columns and rows will add to the same number.

A. RELUCTANTLY
B. TORMENTED
C. MAKESHIFT
D. WEARY
E. INDEBTED
F. INTENT
G. FRAYED
H. MESMERIZED
I. CONDOLENCES
J. DROWSY
K. JALOPY
L. VENOM
M. AMBUSHED
N. PENETRATE
O. TORRENT
P. DEPORTATIONS

1. Experiencing intense pain, especially mental pain
2. Worn away or tattered along the edges
3. Falling-apart automobile
4. Pierce or pass into or through
5. Attacked from a hidden position
6. Poison
7. Spellbound; fascinated
8. Unwillingly; disinclined
9. Lawful removal of illegal immigrants
10. Expressions of sympathy for a person who is suffering sorrow, misfortune or grief
11. Owing for favors or kindness received
12. Tired
13. Made from whatever materials are available rather than usual means
14. Sharply focused on something
15. Sleepy
16. Stream of water flowing with great speed, force & violence

A=	B=	C=	D=
E=	F=	G=	H=
I=	J=	K=	L=
M=	N=	O=	P=

Esperanza Rising Vocabulary Magic Squares 1 Answer Key

Match the definition with the vocabulary word. Put your answers in the magic squares below. When your answers are correct, all columns and rows will add to the same number.

A. RELUCTANTLY
B. TORMENTED
C. MAKESHIFT
D. WEARY
E. INDEBTED
F. INTENT
G. FRAYED
H. MESMERIZED
I. CONDOLENCES
J. DROWSY
K. JALOPY
L. VENOM
M. AMBUSHED
N. PENETRATE
O. TORRENT
P. DEPORTATIONS

1. Experiencing intense pain, especially mental pain
2. Worn away or tattered along the edges
3. Falling-apart automobile
4. Pierce or pass into or through
5. Attacked from a hidden position
6. Poison
7. Spellbound; fascinated
8. Unwillingly; disinclined
9. Lawful removal of illegal immigrants
10. Expressions of sympathy for a person who is suffering sorrow, misfortune or grief
11. Owing for favors or kindness received
12. Tired
13. Made from whatever materials are available rather than usual means
14. Sharply focused on something
15. Sleepy
16. Stream of water flowing with great speed, force & violence

A=8	B=1	C=13	D=12
E=11	F=14	G=2	H=7
I=10	J=15	K=3	L=6
M=5	N=4	O=16	P=9

Esperanza Rising Vocabulary Magic Squares 2

Match the definition with the vocabulary word. Put your answers in the magic squares below. When your answers are correct, all columns and rows will add to the same number.

A. GINGERLY
B. INDEBTED
C. EXTRAVAGANT
D. YEARNING
E. DEBRIS
F. TORRENT
G. SUPPLENESS
H. SCYTHE
I. INFURIATED
J. SQUALOR
K. ERUPTED
L. WEARY
M. CONDOLENCES
N. ACCUSTOMED
O. RELAPSE
P. SERENADED

1. Return of a disease or illness after partial recovery from it
2. Unsatisfied desire
3. Condition of filth and misery
4. Remains of anything broken down or destroyed; ruins; rubble
5. Very angry
6. Stream of water flowing with great speed, force & violence
7. Entertained with a musical performance, esp. by a lover under the window of his sweetheart
8. Tending towards extreme or excessive spending
9. Tool with a long, single-edged blade set at an angle for cutting grass or grain
10. Emerged violently
11. With great care or caution
12. Being in the habit of
13. Owing for favors or kindness received
14. Expressions of sympathy for a person who is suffering sorrow, misfortune or grief
15. Flexibility
16. Tired

A= 11	B= 13	C= 8	D= 2
E= 4	F= 6	G= 15	H= 9
I= 5	J= 3	K= 10	L= 16
M= 14	N= 12	O= 1	P= 7

Esperanza Rising Vocabulary Magic Squares 2 Answer Key

Match the definition with the vocabulary word. Put your answers in the magic squares below. When your answers are correct, all columns and rows will add to the same number.

A. GINGERLY
B. INDEBTED
C. EXTRAVAGANT
D. YEARNING
E. DEBRIS
F. TORRENT
G. SUPPLENESS
H. SCYTHE
I. INFURIATED
J. SQUALOR
K. ERUPTED
L. WEARY
M. CONDOLENCES
N. ACCUSTOMED
O. RELAPSE
P. SERENADED

1. Return of a disease or illness after partial recovery from it
2. Unsatisfied desire
3. Condition of filth and misery
4. Remains of anything broken down or destroyed; ruins; rubble
5. Very angry
6. Stream of water flowing with great speed, force & violence
7. Entertained with a musical performance, esp. by a lover under the window of his sweetheart
8. Tending towards extreme or excessive spending
9. Tool with a long, single-edged blade set at an angle for cutting grass or grain
10. Emerged violently
11. With great care or caution
12. Being in the habit of
13. Owing for favors or kindness received
14. Expressions of sympathy for a person who is suffering sorrow, misfortune or grief
15. Flexibility
16. Tired

A=11	B=13	C=8	D=2
E=4	F=6	G=15	H=9
I=5	J=3	K=10	L=16
M=14	N=12	O=1	P=7

Esperanza Rising Vocabulary Magic Squares 3

Match the definition with the vocabulary word. Put your answers in the magic squares below. When your answers are correct, all columns and rows will add to the same number.

A. TAUT
B. CAPRICIOUS
C. CONDOLENCES
D. MUSSED
E. DOTING
F. MONOTONOUS
G. ERUPTED
H. RETRIEVED
I. SERENADED
J. EXTRAVAGANT
K. INFURIATED
L. BROODED
M. BUOYED
N. SALVAGE
O. TORMENTED
P. RIVETED

1. Tightly drawn; tense
2. Saving something from fire, danger, etc.
3. Tending towards extreme or excessive spending
4. Being excessively fond of
5. Emerged violently
6. Was in a state of gloomy, serious thought
7. Fastened (the eye, attention, etc.) firmly to something
8. Expressions of sympathy for a person who is suffering sorrow, misfortune or grief
9. Experiencing intense pain, especially mental pain
10. Messy or untidy; rumpled
11. Recovered or regained
12. Very angry
13. Entertained with a musical performance, esp. by a lover under the window of his sweetheart
14. Lacking in variety; boring
15. Tending to change abruptly without apparent reason
16. Heartened or inspired; uplifted

A=	B=	C=	D=
E=	F=	G=	H=
I=	J=	K=	L=
M=	N=	O=	P=

Esperanza Rising Vocabulary Magic Squares 3 Answer Key

Match the definition with the vocabulary word. Put your answers in the magic squares below. When your answers are correct, all columns and rows will add to the same number.

A. TAUT
B. CAPRICIOUS
C. CONDOLENCES
D. MUSSED
E. DOTING
F. MONOTONOUS
G. ERUPTED
H. RETRIEVED
I. SERENADED
J. EXTRAVAGANT
K. INFURIATED
L. BROODED
M. BUOYED
N. SALVAGE
O. TORMENTED
P. RIVETED

1. Tightly drawn; tense
2. Saving something from fire, danger, etc.
3. Tending towards extreme or excessive spending
4. Being excessively fond of
5. Emerged violently
6. Was in a state of gloomy, serious thought
7. Fastened (the eye, attention, etc.) firmly to something
8. Expressions of sympathy for a person who is suffering sorrow, misfortune or grief
9. Experiencing intense pain, especially mental pain
10. Messy or untidy; rumpled
11. Recovered or regained
12. Very angry
13. Entertained with a musical performance, esp. by a lover under the window of his sweetheart
14. Lacking in variety; boring
15. Tending to change abruptly without apparent reason
16. Heartened or inspired; uplifted

A=1	B=15	C=8	D=10
E=4	F=14	G=5	H=11
I=13	J=3	K=12	L=6
M=16	N=2	O=9	P=7

Esperanza Rising Vocabulary Magic Squares 4

Match the definition with the vocabulary word. Put your answers in the magic squares below. When your answers are correct, all columns and rows will add to the same number.

A. AMBUSHED
B. SALVAGE
C. INDEBTED
D. MESMERIZED
E. MONOTONOUS
F. MUSSED
G. INTENT
H. BROODED
I. FRANTICALLY
J. DWINDLED
K. ANTICIPATED
L. TAUT
M. CORDIAL
N. DEPORTATIONS
O. CONDOLENCES
P. EXTRAVAGANT

1. Was in a state of gloomy, serious thought
2. Attacked from a hidden position
3. Saving something from fire, danger, etc.
4. Sharply focused on something
5. Made smaller or less
6. Expressions of sympathy for a person who is suffering sorrow, misfortune or grief
7. Tending towards extreme or excessive spending
8. Characterized by rapid and disordered or nervous activity
9. Looked forward to; expected
10. Lawful removal of illegal immigrants
11. Friendly; warm
12. Tightly drawn; tense
13. Lacking in variety; boring
14. Spellbound; fascinated
15. Owing for favors or kindness received
16. Messy or untidy; rumpled

A=	B=	C=	D=
E=	F=	G=	H=
I=	J=	K=	L=
M=	N=	O=	P=

Esperanza Rising Vocabulary Magic Squares 4 Answer Key

Match the definition with the vocabulary word. Put your answers in the magic squares below. When your answers are correct, all columns and rows will add to the same number.

A. AMBUSHED
B. SALVAGE
C. INDEBTED
D. MESMERIZED
E. MONOTONOUS
F. MUSSED
G. INTENT
H. BROODED
I. FRANTICALLY
J. DWINDLED
K. ANTICIPATED
L. TAUT
M. CORDIAL
N. DEPORTATIONS
O. CONDOLENCES
P. EXTRAVAGANT

1. Was in a state of gloomy, serious thought
2. Attacked from a hidden position
3. Saving something from fire, danger, etc.
4. Sharply focused on something
5. Made smaller or less
6. Expressions of sympathy for a person who is suffering sorrow, misfortune or grief
7. Tending towards extreme or excessive spending
8. Characterized by rapid and disordered or nervous activity
9. Looked forward to; expected
10. Lawful removal of illegal immigrants
11. Friendly; warm
12. Tightly drawn; tense
13. Lacking in variety; boring
14. Spellbound; fascinated
15. Owing for favors or kindness received
16. Messy or untidy; rumpled

A=2	B=3	C=15	D=14
E=13	F=16	G=4	H=1
I=8	J=5	K=9	L=12
M=11	N=10	O=6	P=7

Esperanza Rising Vocabulary Word Search 1

```
T Z Y B P M D F N T Y C A S C A D E
F T J B K E U R R O L F V P T C P N
B P S H D F O S S R F S S E P C C M
Z U U O L C T K S R D L S W G O O B
D R O W S Y C O P E S K E I N S T D
D R I Y M B R P L N D T N N S T N X
B O C F E L T E T A G E G T I A T
V C I K X D V G N R E D L S R N N F
F O R L O R N V T R E C P C I G N L
W G P B A I B E L Z F K P Y K R A F
N Z A M C W N Y I N P D U T E O T C
J Y C A O E F R V W V F S H T N S C
N A N L P N E D E T P U R E G A L J
K E L N Z M H A N L M K O A B E U P
M A X O S Z R M O D J D P Y Y M G T
T P T E P Y X D M R E L A P S E K G
D G M J W Y D E B R I S V F P D D R
```

Approaching boldly or aggressively (9)
Conduct; behavior; manner (8)
Emerged violently (7)
Face and deal with responsibilities, problems, or difficulties (4)
Falling-apart automobile (6)
Flexibility (10)
Grand; fit for royalty (5)
Guilty of dishonest practices; untrustworthy (7)
Heartened or inspired; uplifted (6)
Lengths of thread or yarn wound in a loose coil (6)
Light, portable bed, esp. one of canvas on a folding frame (3)
Lonely and sad; unhappy and neglected (7)
Looked at with wonder, admiration, or shock (8)
Messy or untidy; rumpled (6)
Not flowing or running, as water, air, etc. (8)
Pierce or pass into or through (9)
Poison (5)
Refuse to do work because of a disagreement with an employer over pay or conditions (6)
Remains of anything broken down or destroyed; ruins; rubble (6)

Return of a disease or illness after partial recovery from it (7)
Rush down in large amounts (7)
Shooting out forcefully, usually in an uncontrolled manner (7)
Sleepy (6)
Solid fat taken from animals used for making candles, soaps, etc. (6)
Spellbound; fascinated (10)
Stream of water flowing with great speed, force & violence (7)
Tending to change abruptly without apparent reason (10)
Threatening to cause evil, harm, or injury (8)
Tightly drawn; tense (4)
Tired (5)
Tool with a long, single-edged blade set at an angle for cutting grass or grain (6)
Treat or regard with disrespect or shame (5)
Visible breath, as fog, mist, steam, smoke, or gas (6)
Was in a state of gloomy, serious thought (7)
With great care or caution (8)
Worn away or tattered along the edges (6)

Esperanza Rising Vocabulary Word Search 1 Answer Key

Approaching boldly or aggressively (9)
Conduct; behavior; manner (8)
Emerged violently (7)
Face and deal with responsibilities, problems, or difficulties (4)
Falling-apart automobile (6)
Flexibility (10)
Grand; fit for royalty (5)
Guilty of dishonest practices; untrustworthy (7)
Heartened or inspired; uplifted (6)
Lengths of thread or yarn wound in a loose coil (6)
Light, portable bed, esp. one of canvas on a folding frame (3)
Lonely and sad; unhappy and neglected (7)
Looked at with wonder, admiration, or shock (8)
Messy or untidy; rumpled (6)
Not flowing or running, as water, air, etc. (8)
Pierce or pass into or through (9)
Poison (5)
Refuse to do work because of a disagreement with an employer over pay or conditions (6)
Remains of anything broken down or destroyed; ruins; rubble (6)
Return of a disease or illness after partial recovery from it (7)
Rush down in large amounts (7)
Shooting out forcefully, usually in an uncontrolled manner (7)
Sleepy (6)
Solid fat taken from animals used for making candles, soaps, etc. (6)
Spellbound; fascinated (10)
Stream of water flowing with great speed, force & violence (7)
Tending to change abruptly without apparent reason (10)
Threatening to cause evil, harm, or injury (8)
Tightly drawn; tense (4)
Tired (5)
Tool with a long, single-edged blade set at an angle for cutting grass or grain (6)
Treat or regard with disrespect or shame (5)
Visible breath, as fog, mist, steam, smoke, or gas (6)
Was in a state of gloomy, serious thought (7)
With great care or caution (8)
Worn away or tattered along the edges (6)

Esperanza Rising Vocabulary Word Search 2

```
E X T R A V A G A N T L G T T G S G
R T A U N T I N G S Q W N C K Q F P
U Z D O T I N G S D D Z I C O Q R T
P S S E C N E L O D N O C L P V A Q
T T E G W D R E L U C T A N T L Y N
E A S N I E K S E Y D N N N I E E B
D G P R Q B D G M Y R A E W M S D F
F N A H R T D C N O K T M G I C E S
V A L I S E D E L D N I W D S O V W
Y N E G D D G R Y I E X D T M R O H
W T R O G L O A T J J B R K X T U W
M V O W T F E M I L W A I R T H E T Y
X R E C L I N I N G K L C I A D L N
B D K N O R I T N E R R O T S U Y H
C O P E O T R D R O W S Y P B M T X
Y J B C R M H S A L V A G E Y K Y R
M U S S E D S P R E O C C U P I E D
```

Being excessively fond of (6)
Characteristic in which someone looks on the positive side of things (8)
Completely lost in thought (11)
Emerged violently (7)
Expressing devotion or faith (8)
Expressions of sympathy for a person who is suffering sorrow, misfortune or grief (11)
Face and deal with responsibilities, problems, or difficulties (4)
Falling-apart automobile (6)
Grand; fit for royalty (5)
Leaning back (9)
Lengths of thread or yarn wound in a loose coil (6)
Light, portable bed, esp. one of canvas on a folding frame (3)
Limp; drooped; sagging or falling over (6)
Lonely and sad; unhappy and neglected (7)
Made smaller or less (8)
Messy or untidy; rumpled (6)
Not flowing or running, as water, air, etc. (8)
Owing for favors or kindness received (8)
Poison (5)
Refuse to do work because of a disagreement with an employer over pay or conditions (6)

Remains of anything broken down or destroyed; ruins; rubble (6)
Return of a disease or illness after partial recovery from it (7)
Saving something from fire, danger, etc. (7)
Seriously (8)
Sharply focused on something (6)
Sleepy (6)
Small piece of luggage (6)
Stream of water flowing with great speed, force & violence (7)
Structure or place blessed or devoted to some holy person (6)
Teasing (8)
Tending towards extreme or excessive spending (11)
Threatening to cause evil, harm, or injury (8)
Tightly drawn; tense (4)
Tired (5)
Treat or regard with disrespect or shame (5)
Unwillingly; disinclined (11)
Was in a state of gloomy, serious thought (7)
Went along with to protect or aid (8)
Worn away or tattered along the edges (6)

Esperanza Rising Vocabulary Word Search 2 Answer Key

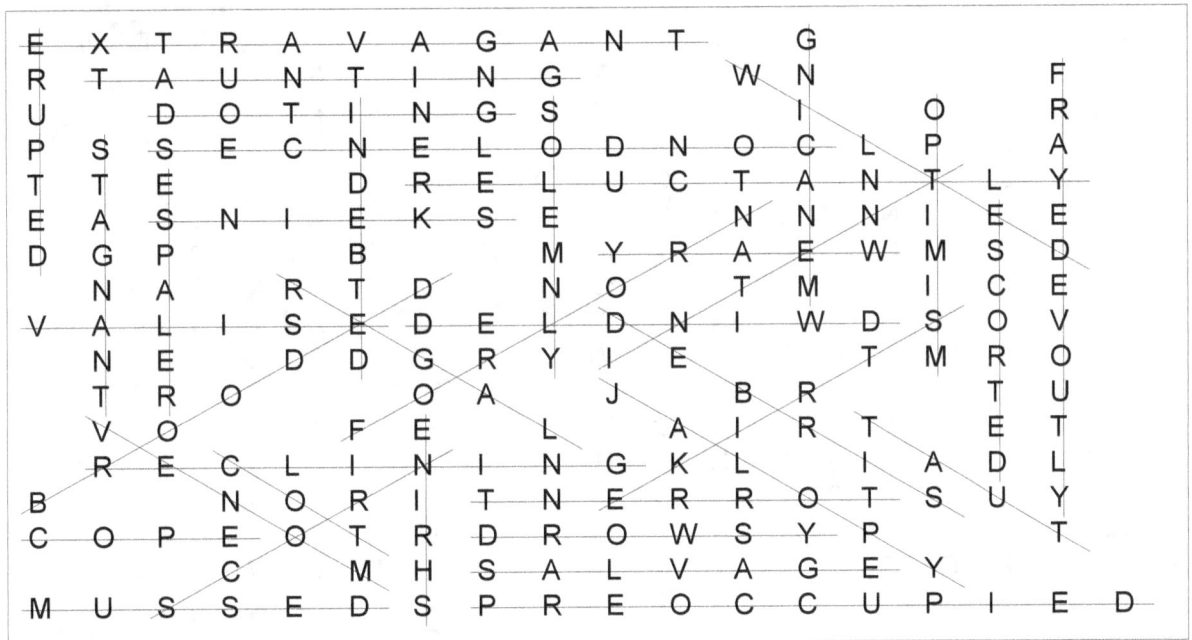

Being excessively fond of (6)
Characteristic in which someone looks on the positive side of things (8)
Completely lost in thought (11)
Emerged violently (7)
Expressing devotion or faith (8)
Expressions of sympathy for a person who is suffering sorrow, misfortune or grief (11)
Face and deal with responsibilities, problems, or difficulties (4)
Falling-apart automobile (6)
Grand; fit for royalty (5)
Leaning back (9)
Lengths of thread or yarn wound in a loose coil (6)
Light, portable bed, esp. one of canvas on a folding frame (3)
Limp; drooped; sagging or falling over (6)
Lonely and sad; unhappy and neglected (7)
Made smaller or less (8)
Messy or untidy; rumpled (6)
Not flowing or running, as water, air, etc. (8)
Owing for favors or kindness received (8)
Poison (5)
Refuse to do work because of a disagreement with an employer over pay or conditions (6)
Remains of anything broken down or destroyed; ruins; rubble (6)
Return of a disease or illness after partial recovery from it (7)
Saving something from fire, danger, etc. (7)
Seriously (8)
Sharply focused on something (6)
Sleepy (6)
Small piece of luggage (6)
Stream of water flowing with great speed, force & violence (7)
Structure or place blessed or devoted to some holy person (6)
Teasing (8)
Tending towards extreme or excessive spending (11)
Threatening to cause evil, harm, or injury (8)
Tightly drawn; tense (4)
Tired (5)
Treat or regard with disrespect or shame (5)
Unwillingly; disinclined (11)
Was in a state of gloomy, serious thought (7)
Went along with to protect or aid (8)
Worn away or tattered along the edges (6)

Esperanza Rising Vocabulary Word Search 3

```
Y E A R N I N G J W Y S W O R D H N D V
C C Q S M L L P A C E W G M E E Z X E T
T A U N T I N G L X M A K E S H I F T K
N P R M Q R V B O A T D R L O S G O N C
E R B E Q L I M P S I O L Y U U C K E R
D I C E E N C K Y H C T F J N B F O M X
N C O D S N T N E T N I E D D M R D R D
O I R E P T I X L W G N Y D I A A E O N
P O R L A D O N A X I G A K N X Y B T V
S U U E L E W W G M W L N Q G T E R S P
E S P V E P E N E T R A T E D V D I U L
D O T R R O U V R D K N I E E A E S O D
C T S A Y R S N H M E E C R D L S N N B
F H J M D T S H G R V R I I O I S C O J
O S R O P A V Z R E X U P V O S U A T M
R Y K X B T S O J I N P A E R E M S O F
L K J E D I T X L T N T T B K K C N D
O J P P I O R X F A X E E E V R K A O F
R E C L I N I N G U W D D D X Z D D M C
N W X L S S S C Y T H E S C O R T E D N
```

AMBUSHED	ESCORTED	RIVETED
ANTICIPATED	FORLORN	SCORN
BESTOWED	FRAYED	SCYTHE
BROODED	INTENT	SHRINE
CAPRICIOUS	JALOPY	SKEINS
CAREENING	MAKESHIFT	STRIKE
CASCADE	MARVELED	TAUNTING
COPE	MONOTONOUS	TAUT
CORRUPT	MUSSED	TORMENTED
COT	PENETRATE	TORRENT
DEBRIS	PLAITED	VALISE
DEPORTATIONS	PUNGENT	VAPORS
DESPONDENT	RECLINING	VENOM
DOTING	REGAL	WEARY
DROWSY	RELAPSE	WILTED
ERUPTED	RESOUNDING	YEARNING

Esperanza Rising Vocabulary Word Search 3 Answer Key

```
Y E A R N I N G   J   W Y S W O R D       D
C C       S       P A     E       E E     E
T A U N T I N G   M A K E S H I F T       T
N P R       R     O   A   D R     O   O   N
E R B     E       P   I   O T     U C     E
D I C   E E       K   Y   T       N B F   M
N C O D S   N T N E T N I E       D M R   R
O I R E P T I     L W   N   D I   A Y E   O
P O R L A D O N A   W   G   A N   N E B   T
S U U E L   E     W G   L       G   R S   S
E S P V R   P E N E T R A T E D V D I   U
D O T R R   O     U R D   N I E E A E   O
C   R A R   U     N   E   E C R D L S   N
F     M T   N     H G R   E R I O I S   O
O   S R O P A V   R       U P V O   U M T M
R   K   T     T     O   I P A E R   M S O
L     E A     I     T   N T T T B     C N
O         I   O       T A   E E           A
R E C L I N I N G   U   D D D         D   M
N         S   C Y T H E S C O R T E D
```

AMBUSHED	ESCORTED	RIVETED
ANTICIPATED	FORLORN	SCORN
BESTOWED	FRAYED	SCYTHE
BROODED	INTENT	SHRINE
CAPRICIOUS	JALOPY	SKEINS
CAREENING	MAKESHIFT	STRIKE
CASCADE	MARVELED	TAUNTING
COPE	MONOTONOUS	TAUT
CORRUPT	MUSSED	TORMENTED
COT	PENETRATE	TORRENT
DEBRIS	PLAITED	VALISE
DEPORTATIONS	PUNGENT	VAPORS
DESPONDENT	RECLINING	VENOM
DOTING	REGAL	WEARY
DROWSY	RELAPSE	WILTED
ERUPTED	RESOUNDING	YEARNING

Esperanza Rising Vocabulary Word Search 4

```
M S P S C S K E I N S S T E R U P T E D
A C L O G O W E A R Y H A O F R A Y T E D
R Y A L N E R Q S D N R C N R V Q T V D
V T I E I T F R P E M I C P M R A Y X L
E H T M C A D D U S E N O U O U E I G F
L E E N A R E L A P S S I N T E N T M
E G D L N T Y G O O T S T T E F I F T R
D L E Y E E O C P N E C I Q V W I U R L
D W K V M N U T R D D N N Y E H C R E V
V W I V P E B Y D E G D G P S R T I G P
N R R N G P S Y T N S S E M O N A A V
Y R T D D W D B V T R E K C P N E T L M
C E S K O L E D F W B A G D V A M E A G
S C O R N D E E C O M T U A T E T D I W
J L D F N O K D A L R P V F D M N Z D L
X I H I X T S O S L J L E A Q E E S R J
F N W F T I S O C A Z R O Z P D S N O Z
S I C O V N J R A T E N Y R B O E V C S
N N C G C G R B D B D E D A N E R E S Z
E G A V L A S D E T L I W V A L I S E S
```

ACCOSTING	DWINDLED	RECLINING	SPEWING
BEREFT	ERUPTED	REGAL	STRIKE
BROODED	FORLORN	RELAPSE	TALLOW
BUOYED	FRAYED	RENEGADES	TAUNTING
CASCADE	INDEBTED	RESENTMENT	TAUT
COPE	INFURIATED	RIVETED	TORRENT
CORDIAL	INTENT	SALVAGE	VALISE
CORRUPT	MAKESHIFT	SCORN	VAPORS
COT	MARVELED	SCYTHE	VENOM
DEMEANOR	MENACING	SERENADED	WEARY
DESPONDENT	MUSSED	SHRINE	WILTED
DOTING	PENETRATE	SKEINS	
DROWSY	PLAITED	SOLEMNLY	

Esperanza Rising Vocabulary Word Search 4 Answer Key

ACCOSTING	DWINDLED	RECLINING	SPEWING
BEREFT	ERUPTED	REGAL	STRIKE
BROODED	FORLORN	RELAPSE	TALLOW
BUOYED	FRAYED	RENEGADES	TAUNTING
CASCADE	INDEBTED	RESENTMENT	TAUT
COPE	INFURIATED	RIVETED	TORRENT
CORDIAL	INTENT	SALVAGE	VALISE
CORRUPT	MAKESHIFT	SCORN	VAPORS
COT	MARVELED	SCYTHE	VENOM
DEMEANOR	MENACING	SERENADED	WEARY
DESPONDENT	MUSSED	SHRINE	WILTED
DOTING	PENETRATE	SKEINS	
DROWSY	PLAITED	SOLEMNLY	

Esperanza Rising Vocabulary Crossword 1

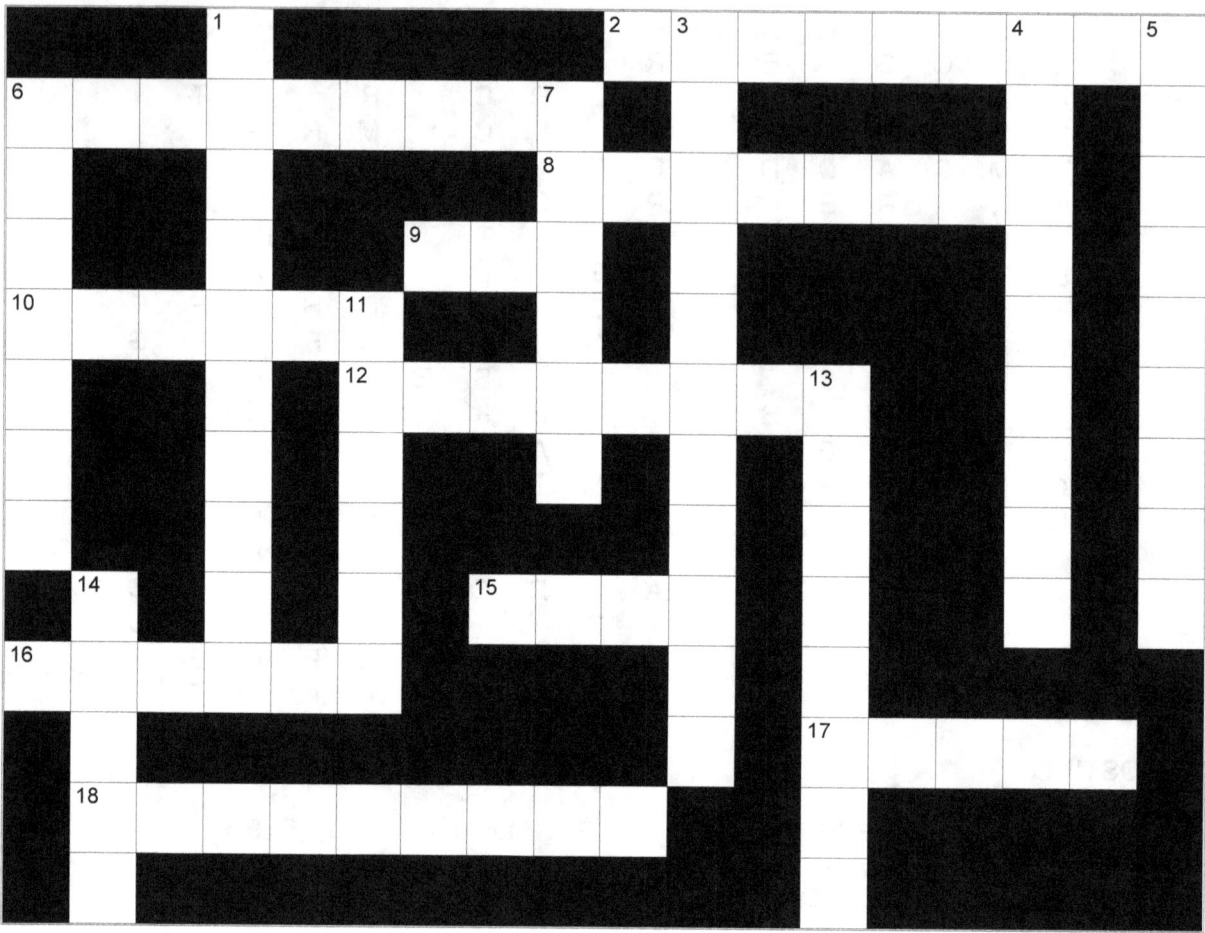

Across
2. Made from whatever materials are available rather than usual means
6. Entertained with a musical performance, esp. by a lover under the window of his sweetheart
8. Characteristic in which someone looks on the positive side of things
9. Light, portable bed, esp. one of canvas on a folding frame
10. Visible breath, as fog, mist, steam, smoke, or gas
12. Teasing
15. Tightly drawn; tense
16. Tool with a long, single-edged blade set at an angle for cutting grass or grain
17. Grand; fit for royalty
18. Outlaws; rebels

Down
1. Depressed; gloomy
3. Looked forward to; expected
4. Protected from a disease
5. Experiencing intense pain, especially mental pain
6. Saving something from fire, danger, etc.
7. Being excessively fond of
11. Refuse to do work because of a disagreement with an employer over pay or conditions
13. With great care or caution
14. Treat or regard with disrespect or shame

Esperanza Rising Vocabulary Crossword 1 Answer Key

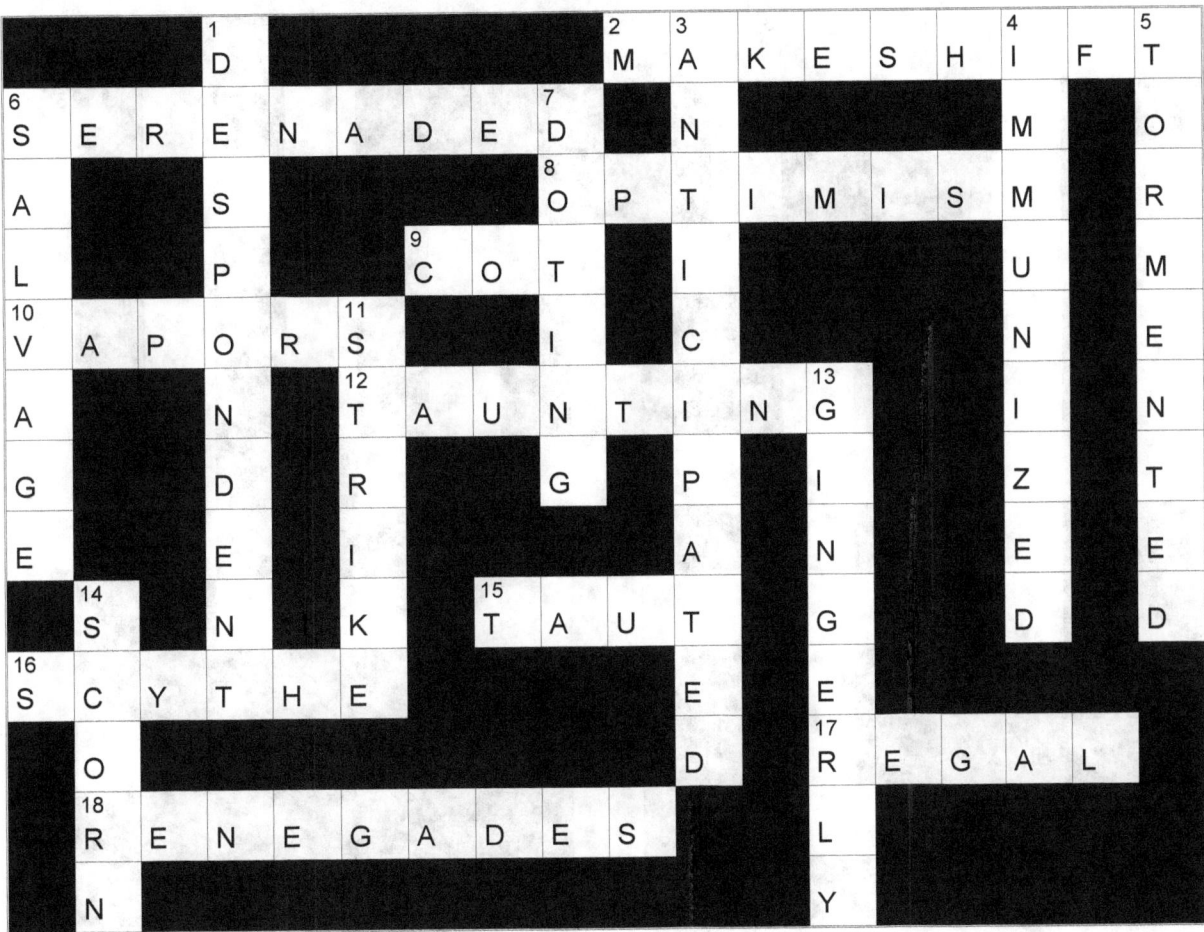

Across
2. Made from whatever materials are available rather than usual means
6. Entertained with a musical performance, esp. by a lover under the window of his sweetheart
8. Characteristic in which someone looks on the positive side of things
9. Light, portable bed, esp. one of canvas on a folding frame
10. Visible breath, as fog, mist, steam, smoke, or gas
12. Teasing
15. Tightly drawn; tense
16. Tool with a long, single-edged blade set at an angle for cutting grass or grain
17. Grand; fit for royalty
18. Outlaws; rebels

Down
1. Depressed; gloomy
3. Looked forward to; expected
4. Protected from a disease
5. Experiencing intense pain, especially mental pain
6. Saving something from fire, danger, etc.
7. Being excessively fond of
11. Refuse to do work because of a disagreement with an employer over pay or conditions
13. With great care or caution
14. Treat or regard with disrespect or shame

Esperanza Rising Vocabulary Crossword 2

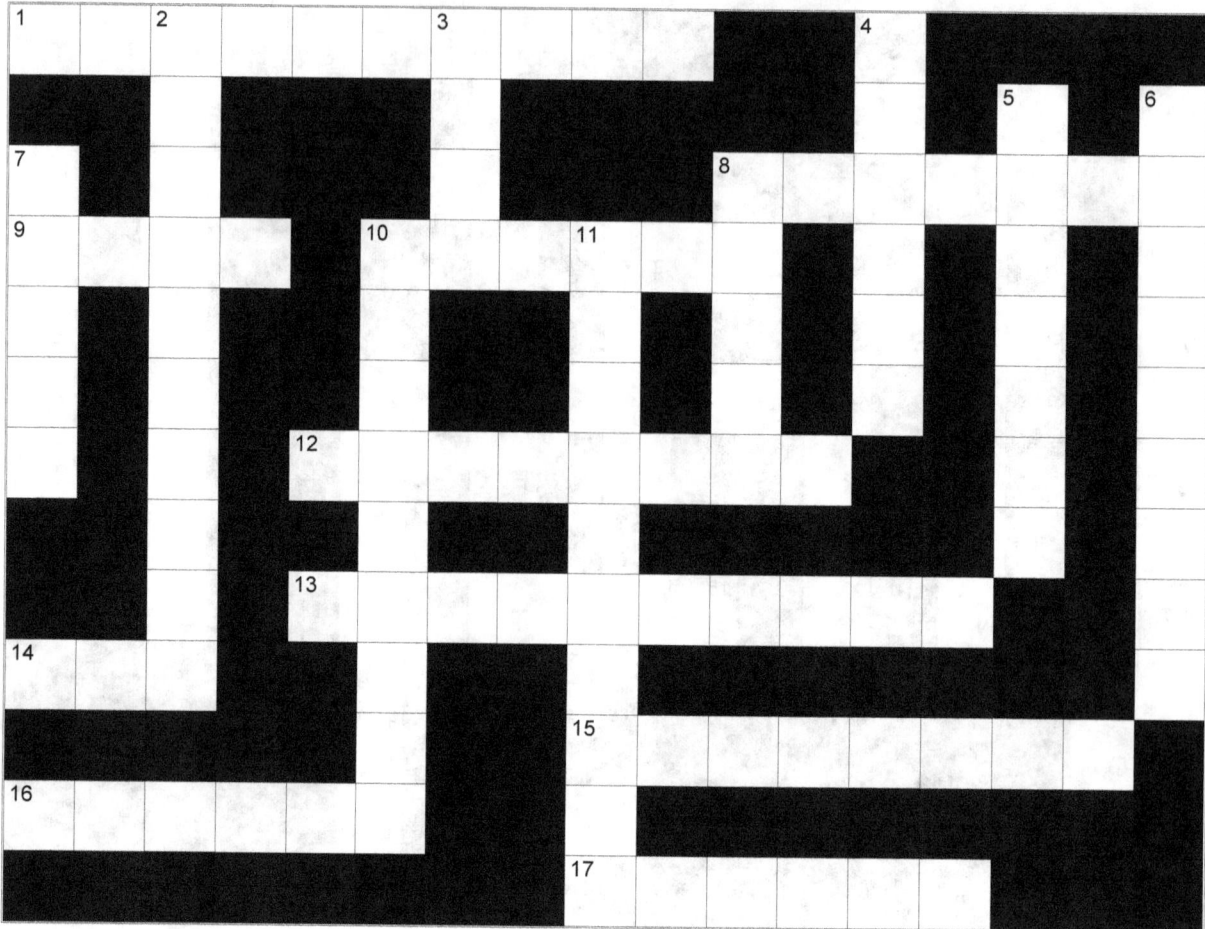

Across
1. Having a wave-like or rippled form or surface
8. Return of a disease or illness after partial recovery from it
9. Face and deal with responsibilities, problems, or difficulties
10. Refuse to do work because of a disagreement with an employer over pay or conditions
12. Expressing devotion or faith
13. Tending to change abruptly without apparent reason
14. Light, portable bed, esp. one of canvas on a folding frame
15. Teasing
16. Heartened or inspired; uplifted
17. Being excessively fond of

Down
2. Depressed; gloomy
3. Tightly drawn; tense
4. Falling-apart automobile
5. Shooting out forcefully, usually in an uncontrolled manner
6. Outlaws; rebels
7. Treat or regard with disrespect or shame
8. Grand; fit for royalty
10. Entertained with a musical performance, esp. by a lover under the window of his sweetheart
11. Very angry

Esperanza Rising Vocabulary Crossword 2 Answer Key

Across
1. Having a wave-like or rippled form or surface
8. Return of a disease or illness after partial recovery from it
9. Face and deal with responsibilities, problems, or difficulties
10. Refuse to do work because of a disagreement with an employer over pay or conditions
12. Expressing devotion or faith
13. Tending to change abruptly without apparent reason
14. Light, portable bed, esp. one of canvas on a folding frame
15. Teasing
16. Heartened or inspired; uplifted
17. Being excessively fond of

Down
2. Depressed; gloomy
3. Tightly drawn; tense
4. Falling-apart automobile
5. Shooting out forcefully, usually in an uncontrolled manner
6. Outlaws; rebels
7. Treat or regard with disrespect or shame
8. Grand; fit for royalty
10. Entertained with a musical performance, esp. by a lover under the window of his sweetheart
11. Very angry

Esperanza Rising Vocabulary Crossword 3

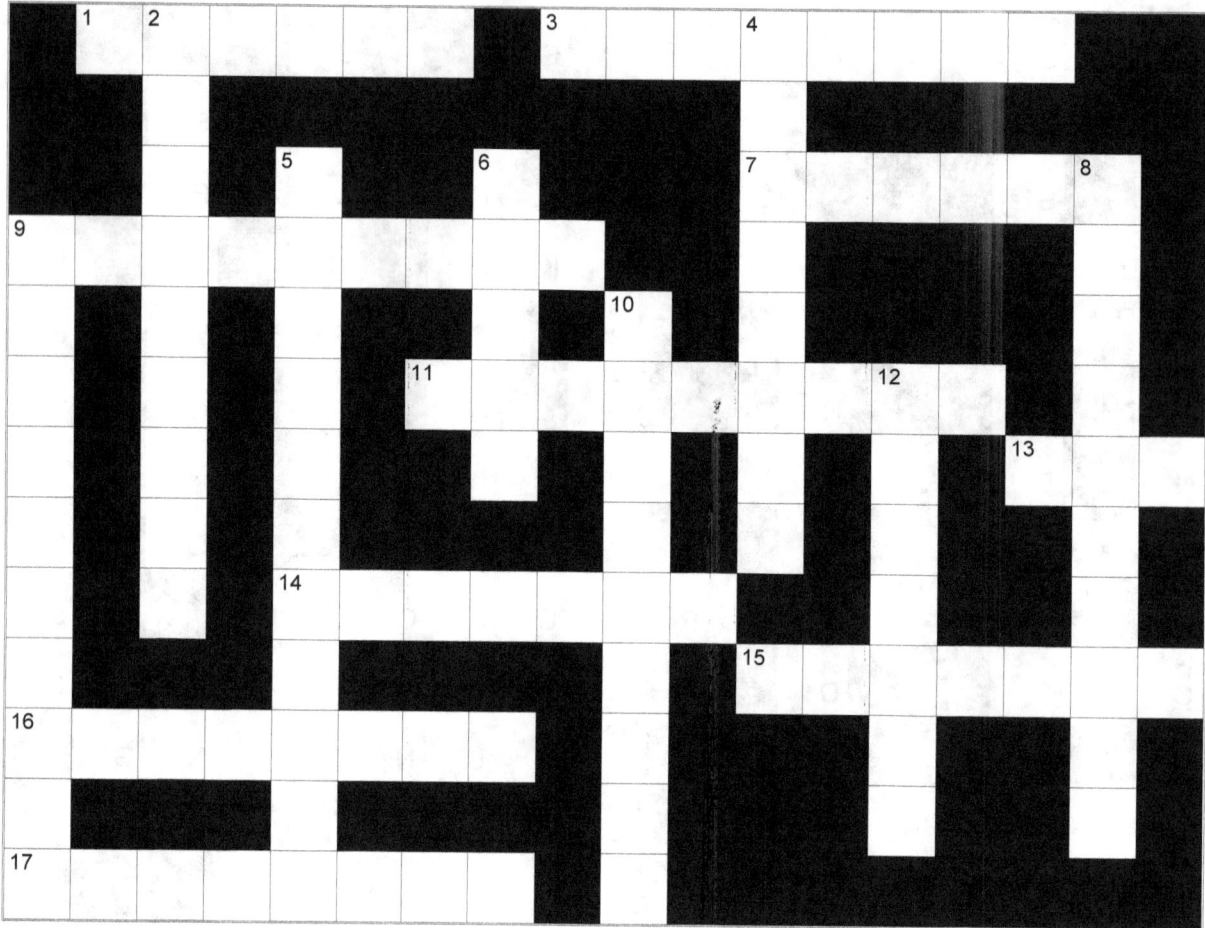

Across
1. Refuse to do work because of a disagreement with an employer over pay or conditions
3. Threatening to cause evil, harm, or injury
7. Heartened or inspired; uplifted
9. Protected from a disease
11. Made from whatever materials are available rather than usual means
13. Light, portable bed, esp. one of canvas on a folding frame
14. Sour or biting in smell or taste
15. Was in a state of gloomy, serious thought
16. Teasing
17. Made smaller or less

Down
2. Experiencing intense pain, especially mental pain
4. Attacked from a hidden position
5. Looked forward to; expected
6. Grand; fit for royalty
8. Depressed; gloomy
9. Very angry
10. Entertained with a musical performance, esp. by a lover under the window of his sweetheart
12. Lonely and sad; unhappy and neglected

Esperanza Rising Vocabulary Crossword 3 Answer Key

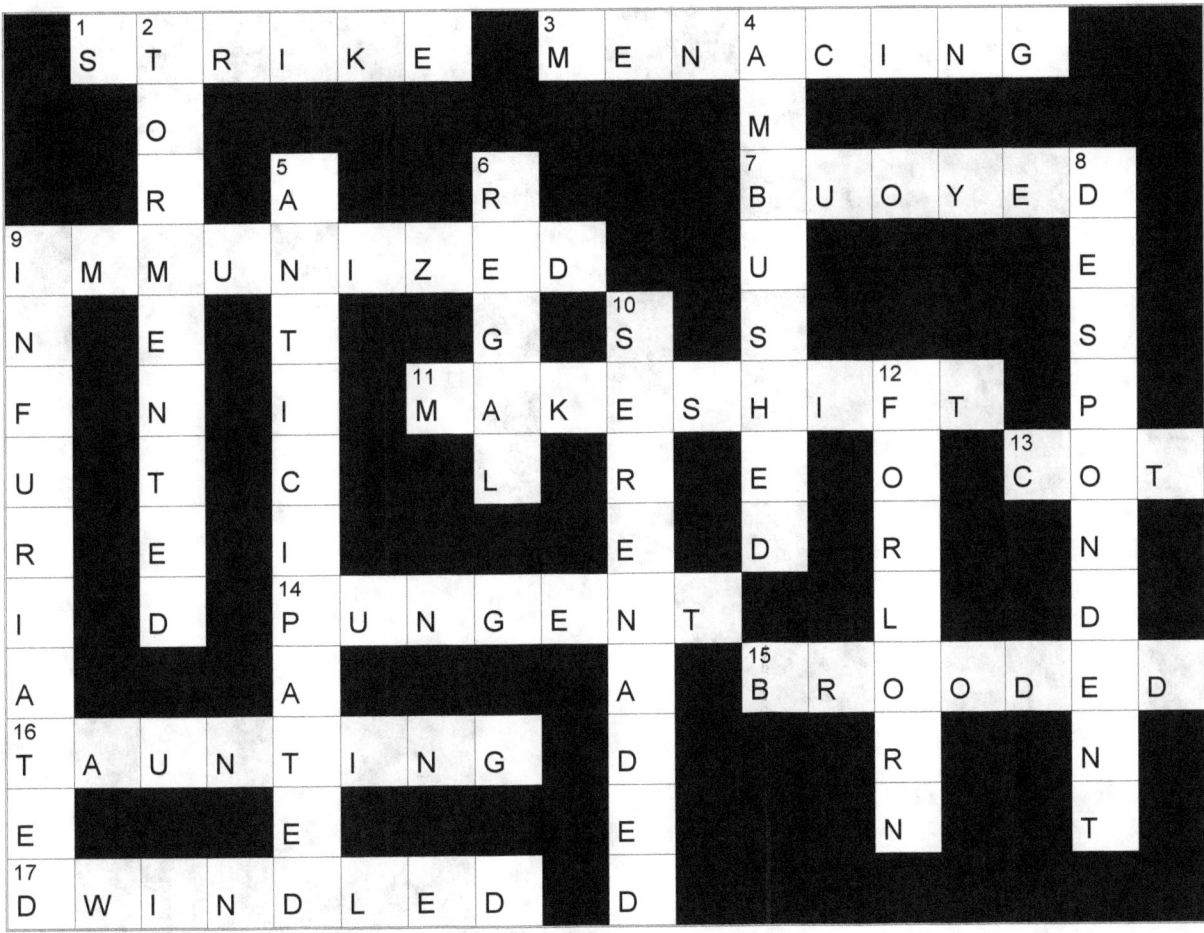

Across
1. Refuse to do work because of a disagreement with an employer over pay or conditions
3. Threatening to cause evil, harm, or injury
7. Heartened or inspired; uplifted
9. Protected from a disease
11. Made from whatever materials are available rather than usual means
13. Light, portable bed, esp. one of canvas on a folding frame
14. Sour or biting in smell or taste
15. Was in a state of gloomy, serious thought
16. Teasing
17. Made smaller or less

Down
2. Experiencing intense pain, especially mental pain
4. Attacked from a hidden position
5. Looked forward to; expected
6. Grand; fit for royalty
8. Depressed; gloomy
9. Very angry
10. Entertained with a musical performance, esp. by a lover under the window of his sweetheart
12. Lonely and sad; unhappy and neglected

Esperanza Rising Vocabulary Crossword 4

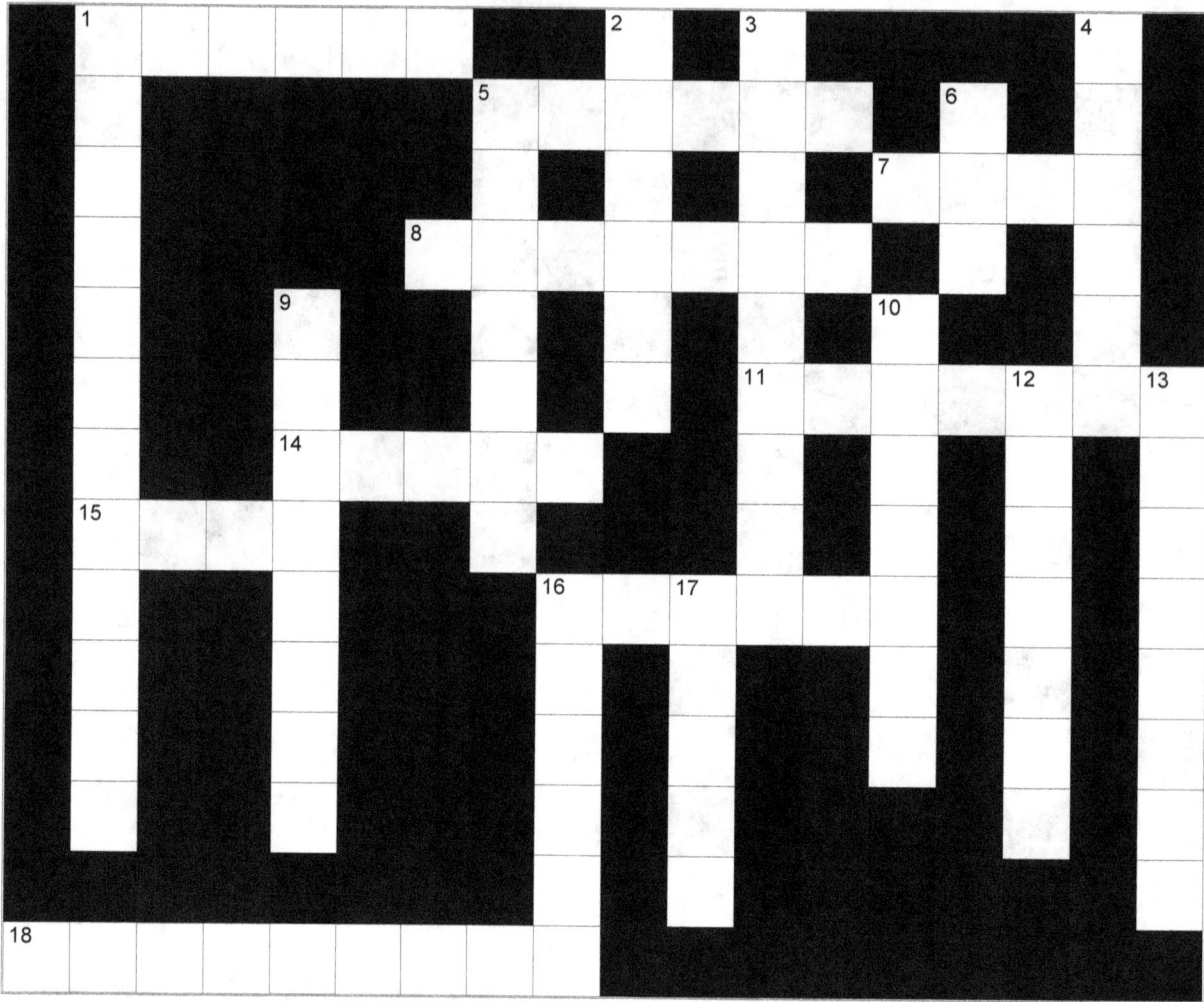

Across
1. Remains of anything broken down or destroyed; ruins; rubble
5. Worn away or tattered along the edges
7. Face and deal with responsibilities, problems, or difficulties
8. Was in a state of gloomy, serious thought
11. Return of a disease or illness after partial recovery from it
14. Treat or regard with disrespect or shame
15. Tightly drawn; tense
16. Without; lacking
18. Protected from a disease

Down
1. Lawful removal of illegal immigrants
2. Falling-apart automobile
3. Pierce or pass into or through
4. Lengths of thread or yarn wound in a loose coil
5. Lonely and sad; unhappy and neglected
6. Light, portable bed, esp. one of canvas on a folding frame
9. Presented as a gift; given
10. Braided
12. Sour or biting in smell or taste
13. Went along with to protect or aid
16. Heartened or inspired; uplifted
17. Grand; fit for royalty

Esperanza Rising Vocabulary Crossword 4 Answer Key

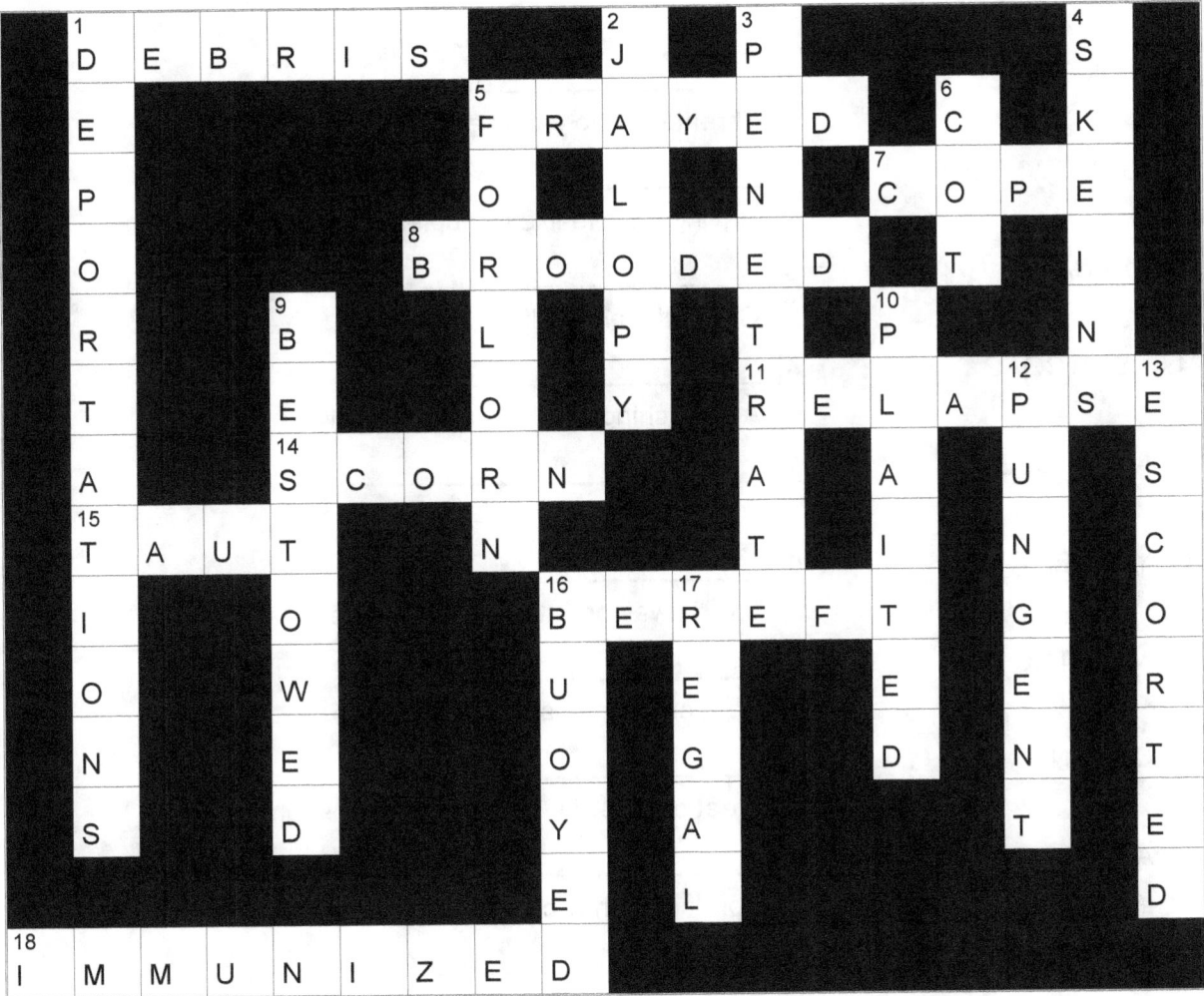

Across
1. Remains of anything broken down or destroyed; ruins; rubble
5. Worn away or tattered along the edges
7. Face and deal with responsibilities, problems, or difficulties
8. Was in a state of gloomy, serious thought
11. Return of a disease or illness after partial recovery from it
14. Treat or regard with disrespect or shame
15. Tightly drawn; tense
16. Without; lacking
18. Protected from a disease

Down
1. Lawful removal of illegal immigrants
2. Falling-apart automobile
3. Pierce or pass into or through
4. Lengths of thread or yarn wound in a loose coil
5. Lonely and sad; unhappy and neglected
6. Light, portable bed, esp. one of canvas on a folding frame
9. Presented as a gift; given
10. Braided
12. Sour or biting in smell or taste
13. Went along with to protect or aid
16. Heartened or inspired; uplifted
17. Grand; fit for royalty

Esperanza Rising Vocabulary Juggle Letters 1

1. NICMGNAE = 1. _____
Threatening to cause evil, harm, or injury

2. IGUNLTANUD = 2. _____
Having a wave-like or rippled form or surface

3. ERLGA = 3. _____
Grand; fit for royalty

4. NSICTCOAG = 4. _____
Approaching boldly or aggressively

5. NPETNDSEDO = 5. _____
Depressed; gloomy

6. YDRAEF = 6. _____
Worn away or tattered along the edges

7. NEPGTNU = 7. _____
Sour or biting in smell or taste

8. OSRCN = 8. _____
Treat or regard with disrespect or shame

9. AENEOMDR = 9. _____
Conduct; behavior; manner

10. EUCPDREPOIC =10. _____
Completely lost in thought

11. ENLYSMLO =11. _____
Seriously

12. CSCTEMOUAD =12. _____
Being in the habit of

13. VDEEIRT =13. _____
Fastened (the eye, attention, etc.) firmly to something

14. PORURTC =14. _____
Guilty of dishonest practices; untrustworthy

Esperanza Rising Vocabulary Juggle Letters 1 Answer Key

1. NICMGNAE = 1. MENACING
   Threatening to cause evil, harm, or injury

2. IGUNLTANUD = 2. UNDULATING
   Having a wave-like or rippled form or surface

3. ERLGA = 3. REGAL
   Grand; fit for royalty

4. NSICTCOAG = 4. ACCOSTING
   Approaching boldly or aggressively

5. NPETNDSEDO = 5. DESPONDENT
   Depressed; gloomy

6. YDRAEF = 6. FRAYED
   Worn away or tattered along the edges

7. NEPGTNU = 7. PUNGENT
   Sour or biting in smell or taste

8. OSRCN = 8. SCORN
   Treat or regard with disrespect or shame

9. AENEOMDR = 9. DEMEANOR
   Conduct; behavior; manner

10. EUCPDREPOIC = 10. PREOCCUPIED
    Completely lost in thought

11. ENLYSMLO = 11. SOLEMNLY
    Seriously

12. CSCTEMOUAD = 12. ACCUSTOMED
    Being in the habit of

13. VDEEIRT = 13. RIVETED
    Fastened (the eye, attention, etc.) firmly to something

14. PORURTC = 14. CORRUPT
    Guilty of dishonest practices; untrustworthy

Esperanza Rising Vocabulary Juggle Letters 2

1. TRSKEI = 1. _____
   Refuse to do work because of a disagreement with an employer over pay or conditions

2. WSDROY = 2. _____
   Sleepy

3. UTNPGEN = 3. _____
   Sour or biting in smell or taste

4. UMEDSS = 4. _____
   Messy or untidy; rumpled

5. POSARV = 5. _____
   Visible breath, as fog, mist, steam, smoke, or gas

6. ZMENIMIDU = 6. _____
   Protected from a disease

7. UMCCDEASTO = 7. _____
   Being in the habit of

8. DEYRFA = 8. _____
   Worn away or tattered along the edges

9. RSDNAEEED = 9. _____
   Entertained with a musical performance, esp. by a lover under the window of his sweetheart

10. YTCHES = 10. _____
    Tool with a long, single-edged blade set at an angle for cutting grass or grain

11. APELESR = 11. _____
    Return of a disease or illness after partial recovery from it

12. DRVTEERIE = 12. _____
    Recovered or regained

13. TPELADI = 13. _____
    Braided

14. OOREDBD = 14. _____
    Was in a state of gloomy, serious thought

Esperanza Rising Vocabulary Juggle Letters 2 Answer Key

1. TRSKEI = 1. STRIKE
Refuse to do work because of a disagreement with an employer over pay or conditions

2. WSDROY = 2. DROWSY
Sleepy

3. UTNPGEN = 3. PUNGENT
Sour or biting in smell or taste

4. UMEDSS = 4. MUSSED
Messy or untidy; rumpled

5. POSARV = 5. VAPORS
Visible breath, as fog, mist, steam, smoke, or gas

6. ZMENIMIDU = 6. IMMUNIZED
Protected from a disease

7. UMCCDEASTO = 7. ACCUSTOMED
Being in the habit of

8. DEYRFA = 8. FRAYED
Worn away or tattered along the edges

9. RSDNAEEED = 9. SERENADED
Entertained with a musical performance, esp. by a lover under the window of his sweetheart

10. YTCHES =10. SCYTHE
Tool with a long, single-edged blade set at an angle for cutting grass or grain

11. APELESR =11. RELAPSE
Return of a disease or illness after partial recovery from it

12. DRVTEERIE =12. RETRIEVED
Recovered or regained

13. TPELADI =13. PLAITED
Braided

14. OOREDBD =14. BROODED
Was in a state of gloomy, serious thought

Esperanza Rising Vocabulary Juggle Letters 3

1. BEHADMUS = 1. _____
   Attacked from a hidden position

2. NVMOE = 2. _____
   Poison

3. NCGIOSATC = 3. _____
   Approaching boldly or aggressively

4. PCRAUCSOII = 4. _____
   Tending to change abruptly without apparent reason

5. OGTIND = 5. _____
   Being excessively fond of

6. TITENN = 6. _____
   Sharply focused on something

7. WTELDI = 7. _____
   Limp; drooped; sagging or falling over

8. CIELEBSTPUS = 8. _____
   Easily influenced; weak

9. ESSNKI = 9. _____
   Lengths of thread or yarn wound in a loose coil

10. ASAEVGL =10. _____
    Saving something from fire, danger, etc.

11. ESDEDENAR =11. _____
    Entertained with a musical performance, esp. by a lover under the window of his sweetheart

12. ERAWY =12. _____
    Tired

13. GMECAINN =13. _____
    Threatening to cause evil, harm, or injury

14. PNIEWGS =14. _____
    Shooting out forcefully, usually in an uncontrolled manner

Esperanza Rising Vocabulary Juggle Letters 3 Answer Key

1. BEHADMUS = 1. AMBUSHED
Attacked from a hidden position

2. NVMOE = 2. VENOM
Poison

3. NCGIOSATC = 3. ACCOSTING
Approaching boldly or aggressively

4. PCRAUCSOII = 4. CAPRICIOUS
Tending to change abruptly without apparent reason

5. OGTIND = 5. DOTING
Being excessively fond of

6. TITENN = 6. INTENT
Sharply focused on something

7. WTELDI = 7. WILTED
Limp; drooped; sagging or falling over

8. CIELEBSTPUS = 8. SUSCEPTIBLE
Easily influenced; weak

9. ESSNKI = 9. SKEINS
Lengths of thread or yarn wound in a loose coil

10. ASAEVGL = 10. SALVAGE
Saving something from fire, danger, etc.

11. ESDEDENAR = 11. SERENADED
Entertained with a musical performance, esp. by a lover under the window of his sweetheart

12. ERAWY = 12. WEARY
Tired

13. GMECAINN = 13. MENACING
Threatening to cause evil, harm, or injury

14. PNIEWGS = 14. SPEWING
Shooting out forcefully, usually in an uncontrolled manner

Esperanza Rising Vocabulary Juggle Letters 4

1. HISTAMKFE = 1. _____
   Made from whatever materials are available rather than usual means

2. OIARCDL = 2. _____
   Friendly; warm

3. DGRINNOUES = 3. _____
   Making an echoing sound

4. AICNSTOCG = 4. _____
   Approaching boldly or aggressively

5. TNAVAAERXGT = 5. _____
   Tending towards extreme or excessive spending

6. INGYNEAR = 6. _____
   Unsatisfied desire

7. ISEVAL = 7. _____
   Small piece of luggage

8. AYFRED = 8. _____
   Worn away or tattered along the edges

9. LNCIGNRIE = 9. _____
   Leaning back

10. IOUPASCRIC =10. _____
    Tending to change abruptly without apparent reason

11. GONTID =11. _____
    Being excessively fond of

12. TSSEIUBEPCL =12. _____
    Easily influenced; weak

13. OVNEM =13. _____
    Poison

14. PROCURT =14. _____
    Guilty of dishonest practices; untrustworthy

Esperanza Rising Vocabulary Juggle Letters 4 Answer Key

1. HISTAMKFE = 1. MAKESHIFT
   Made from whatever materials are available rather than usual means

2. OIARCDL = 2. CORDIAL
   Friendly; warm

3. DGRINNOUES = 3. RESOUNDING
   Making an echoing sound

4. AICNSTOCG = 4. ACCOSTING
   Approaching boldly or aggressively

5. TNAVAAERXGT = 5. EXTRAVAGANT
   Tending towards extreme or excessive spending

6. INGYNEAR = 6. YEARNING
   Unsatisfied desire

7. ISEVAL = 7. VALISE
   Small piece of luggage

8. AYFRED = 8. FRAYED
   Worn away or tattered along the edges

9. LNCIGNRIE = 9. RECLINING
   Leaning back

10. IOUPASCRIC = 10. CAPRICIOUS
    Tending to change abruptly without apparent reason

11. GONTID = 11. DOTING
    Being excessively fond of

12. TSSEIUBEPCL = 12. SUSCEPTIBLE
    Easily influenced; weak

13. OVNEM = 13. VENOM
    Poison

14. PROCURT = 14. CORRUPT
    Guilty of dishonest practices; untrustworthy

ACCOSTING	Approaching boldly or aggressively
ACCUSTOMED	Being in the habit of
AMBUSHED	Attacked from a hidden position
ANTICIPATED	Looked forward to; expected
BEREFT	Without; lacking
BESTOWED	Presented as a gift; given

BROODED	Was in a state of gloomy, serious thought
BUOYED	Heartened or inspired; uplifted
CAPRICIOUS	Tending to change abruptly without apparent reason
CAREENING	Wobbling or swerving while in motion, usually at high speed
CASCADE	Rush down in large amounts
CONDOLENCES	Expressions of sympathy for a person who is suffering sorrow, misfortune or grief

COPE	Face and deal with responsibilities, problems, or difficulties
CORDIAL	Friendly; warm
CORRUPT	Guilty of dishonest practices; untrustworthy
COT	Light, portable bed, esp. one of canvas on a folding frame
DEBRIS	Remains of anything broken down or destroyed; ruins; rubble
DEMEANOR	Conduct; behavior; manner

DEPORTATIONS	Lawful removal of illegal immigrants
DESPONDENT	Depressed; gloomy
DEVOUTLY	Expressing devotion or faith
DOTING	Being excessively fond of
DROWSY	Sleepy
DWINDLED	Made smaller or less

ERUPTED	Emerged violently
ESCORTED	Went along with to protect or aid
EXTRAVAGANT	Tending towards extreme or excessive spending
FORLORN	Lonely and sad; unhappy and neglected
FRANTICALLY	Characterized by rapid and disordered or nervous activity
FRAYED	Worn away or tattered along the edges

GINGERLY	With great care or caution
IMMUNIZED	Protected from a disease
INDEBTED	Owing for favors or kindness received
INFURIATED	Very angry
INTENT	Sharply focused on something
JALOPY	Falling-apart automobile

MAKESHIFT	Made from whatever materials are available rather than usual means
MARVELED	Looked at with wonder, admiration, or shock
MENACING	Threatening to cause evil, harm, or injury
MESMERIZED	Spellbound; fascinated
MONOTONOUS	Lacking in variety; boring
MUSSED	Messy or untidy; rumpled

OPTIMISM	Characteristic in which someone looks on the positive side of things
PENETRATE	Pierce or pass into or through
PERSISTENT	Determined; refusing to give up
PLAITED	Braided
PREOCCUPIED	Completely lost in thought
PUNGENT	Sour or biting in smell or taste

RECLINING	Leaning back
REGAL	Grand; fit for royalty
RELAPSE	Return of a disease or illness after partial recovery from it
RELUCTANTLY	Unwillingly; disinclined
RENEGADES	Outlaws; rebels
RESENTMENT	Feeling of displeasure from a sense of being injured or offended

RESOUNDING	Making an echoing sound
RETRIEVED	Recovered or regained
RIVETED	Fastened (the eye, attention, etc.) firmly to something
SALVAGE	Saving something from fire, danger, etc.
SCORN	Treat or regard with disrespect or shame
SCYTHE	Tool with a long, single-edged blade set at an angle for cutting grass or grain

SERENADED	Entertained with a musical performance, esp. by a lover under the window of his sweetheart
SHRINE	Structure or place blessed or devoted to some holy person
SKEINS	Lengths of thread or yarn wound in a loose coil
SOLEMNLY	Seriously
SPEWING	Shooting out forcefully, usually in an uncontrolled manner
SQUALOR	Condition of filth and misery

STAGNANT	Not flowing or running, as water, air, etc.
STRIKE	Refuse to do work because of a disagreement with an employer over pay or conditions
SUPPLENESS	Flexibility
SUSCEPTIBLE	Easily influenced; weak
TALLOW	Solid fat taken from animals used for making candles, soaps, etc.
TAUNTING	Teasing

TAUT	Tightly drawn; tense
TORMENTED	Experiencing intense pain, especially mental pain
TORRENT	Stream of water flowing with great speed, force & violence
UNDULATING	Having a wave-like or rippled form or surface
VALISE	Small piece of luggage
VAPORS	Visible breath, as fog, mist, steam, smoke, or gas

VENOM	Poison
WEARY	Tired
WILTED	Limp; drooped; sagging or falling over
YEARNING	Unsatisfied desire

Esperanza Rising Vocabulary

WEARY	RESOUNDING	DEBRIS	CORRUPT	ACCUSTOMED
SERENADED	OPTIMISM	RENEGADES	DWINDLED	COPE
SHRINE	IMMUNIZED	FREE SPACE	MARVELED	PUNGENT
RELAPSE	CORDIAL	BUOYED	ESCORTED	FRAYED
PREOCCUPIED	DEMEANOR	RIVETED	ANTICIPATED	SUPPLENESS

Esperanza Rising Vocabulary

MONOTONOUS	SOLEMNLY	RECLINING	VAPORS	CAPRICIOUS
WILTED	RETRIEVED	BROODED	TAUT	PLAITED
JALOPY	SQUALOR	FREE SPACE	TAUNTING	DESPONDENT
DEVOUTLY	MAKESHIFT	GINGERLY	INDEBTED	FORLORN
INFURIATED	TORRENT	PENETRATE	STRIKE	BEREFT

Esperanza Rising Vocabulary

TORRENT	SHRINE	INTENT	PUNGENT	UNDULATING
ERUPTED	RELAPSE	INFURIATED	COT	SPEWING
BESTOWED	PENETRATE	FREE SPACE	BROODED	SKEINS
TAUNTING	STRIKE	DROWSY	IMMUNIZED	MUSSED
PERSISTENT	ACCOSTING	SCYTHE	CASCADE	TORMENTED

Esperanza Rising Vocabulary

PLAITED	VALISE	SUSCEPTIBLE	DWINDLED	GINGERLY
PREOCCUPIED	FORLORN	DEBRIS	MESMERIZED	CORDIAL
WILTED	TAUT	FREE SPACE	SQUALOR	EXTRAVAGANT
COPE	DOTING	DEMEANOR	AMBUSHED	VENOM
SUPPLENESS	RIVETED	OPTIMISM	SCORN	RESENTMENT

Esperanza Rising Vocabulary

PREOCCUPIED	RESOUNDING	PLAITED	CORDIAL	AMBUSHED
FRAYED	RELAPSE	BEREFT	BUOYED	RELUCTANTLY
COPE	EXTRAVAGANT	FREE SPACE	WILTED	STAGNANT
DROWSY	MUSSED	BROODED	STRIKE	SKEINS
ACCUSTOMED	VALISE	RENEGADES	SCORN	OPTIMISM

Esperanza Rising Vocabulary

DOTING	DEMEANOR	CAPRICIOUS	TALLOW	SERENADED
INFURIATED	TAUNTING	SCYTHE	YEARNING	SUPPLENESS
DEBRIS	BESTOWED	FREE SPACE	MESMERIZED	SALVAGE
ESCORTED	JALOPY	DEPORTATIONS	SOLEMNLY	ERUPTED
UNDULATING	VAPORS	PERSISTENT	CORRUPT	INDEBTED

Esperanza Rising Vocabulary

BUOYED	DEBRIS	PLAITED	RETRIEVED	SPEWING
INFURIATED	PERSISTENT	MONOTONOUS	ERUPTED	RENEGADES
SKEINS	RECLINING	FREE SPACE	MENACING	RELUCTANTLY
FRANTICALLY	SUPPLENESS	SCYTHE	FORLORN	VAPORS
OPTIMISM	CASCADE	DOTING	RIVETED	REGAL

Esperanza Rising Vocabulary

CORDIAL	DEPORTATIONS	STRIKE	INDEBTED	BROODED
IMMUNIZED	PENETRATE	ESCORTED	CAPRICIOUS	STAGNANT
COT	WILTED	FREE SPACE	CORRUPT	BEREFT
TAUT	RESOUNDING	GINGERLY	AMBUSHED	JALOPY
RELAPSE	INTENT	YEARNING	SCORN	DEMEANOR

Esperanza Rising Vocabulary

MONOTONOUS	REGAL	SUSCEPTIBLE	ESCORTED	IMMUNIZED
SCYTHE	MARVELED	PLAITED	PUNGENT	PENETRATE
SKEINS	MAKESHIFT	FREE SPACE	JALOPY	SCORN
MESMERIZED	TORRENT	DWINDLED	ACCOSTING	SERENADED
INDEBTED	RESENTMENT	SQUALOR	RESOUNDING	OPTIMISM

Esperanza Rising Vocabulary

COPE	BESTOWED	SHRINE	BEREFT	DEPORTATIONS
DEVOUTLY	ANTICIPATED	BUOYED	GINGERLY	RELUCTANTLY
SPEWING	ACCUSTOMED	FREE SPACE	ERUPTED	TAUT
RECLINING	CAREENING	VALISE	UNDULATING	FRANTICALLY
VAPORS	SALVAGE	CORDIAL	MUSSED	WEARY

Esperanza Rising Vocabulary

TALLOW	DEVOUTLY	CAPRICIOUS	JALOPY	ACCOSTING
MENACING	COT	IMMUNIZED	VALISE	VAPORS
TAUT	DEBRIS	FREE SPACE	BESTOWED	SUSCEPTIBLE
RESOUNDING	DROWSY	ACCUSTOMED	TORRENT	GINGERLY
ANTICIPATED	RECLINING	CONDOLENCES	RENEGADES	COPE

Esperanza Rising Vocabulary

DEPORTATIONS	TAUNTING	MARVELED	RESENTMENT	SOLEMNLY
INFURIATED	SALVAGE	SPEWING	RIVETED	WEARY
WILTED	DESPONDENT	FREE SPACE	STRIKE	YEARNING
CAREENING	STAGNANT	FORLORN	DEMEANOR	PUNGENT
UNDULATING	DOTING	SCORN	PLAITED	MAKESHIFT

Esperanza Rising Vocabulary

CORDIAL	PERSISTENT	ESCORTED	SUPPLENESS	ACCOSTING
MARVELED	AMBUSHED	BUOYED	SPEWING	SERENADED
SQUALOR	TAUNTING	FREE SPACE	OPTIMISM	FRANTICALLY
FRAYED	BROODED	CAPRICIOUS	DOTING	PREOCCUPIED
REGAL	RIVETED	VALISE	WEARY	BEREFT

Esperanza Rising Vocabulary

VENOM	PUNGENT	SALVAGE	SCYTHE	STRIKE
DROWSY	MESMERIZED	ANTICIPATED	RETRIEVED	TAUT
UNDULATING	ERUPTED	FREE SPACE	STAGNANT	TORMENTED
RELAPSE	CORRUPT	MUSSED	IMMUNIZED	DEMEANOR
DEVOUTLY	GINGERLY	SHRINE	SOLEMNLY	YEARNING

Esperanza Rising Vocabulary

TORMENTED	RELAPSE	VAPORS	PENETRATE	PLAITED
INFURIATED	AMBUSHED	CAPRICIOUS	STRIKE	TAUNTING
SERENADED	INDEBTED	FREE SPACE	PUNGENT	ESCORTED
DEBRIS	COT	WEARY	OPTIMISM	GINGERLY
DESPONDENT	MONOTONOUS	ERUPTED	REGAL	SCORN

Esperanza Rising Vocabulary

SOLEMNLY	RESENTMENT	CORRUPT	BEREFT	DEMEANOR
MESMERIZED	STAGNANT	FRAYED	SHRINE	PERSISTENT
TORRENT	SQUALOR	FREE SPACE	CAREENING	BUOYED
RESOUNDING	SUSCEPTIBLE	ANTICIPATED	SALVAGE	VENOM
MAKESHIFT	RECLINING	PREOCCUPIED	YEARNING	ACCOSTING

Esperanza Rising Vocabulary

SUSCEPTIBLE	MARVELED	SERENADED	IMMUNIZED	OPTIMISM
RELAPSE	CAREENING	BUOYED	RESOUNDING	VALISE
REGAL	INTENT	FREE SPACE	DWINDLED	DROWSY
RESENTMENT	RENEGADES	SCORN	RECLINING	ESCORTED
AMBUSHED	SPEWING	ANTICIPATED	MUSSED	RIVETED

Esperanza Rising Vocabulary

YEARNING	COT	TORRENT	BESTOWED	MAKESHIFT
PENETRATE	BROODED	EXTRAVAGANT	JALOPY	DESPONDENT
STRIKE	TAUNTING	FREE SPACE	FRAYED	RETRIEVED
SKEINS	WILTED	MONOTONOUS	SUPPLENESS	PLAITED
INFURIATED	BEREFT	TALLOW	COPE	INDEBTED

Esperanza Rising Vocabulary

VALISE	TAUNTING	STRIKE	ESCORTED	MONOTONOUS
GINGERLY	CAREENING	UNDULATING	SPEWING	ACCUSTOMED
FRAYED	DROWSY	FREE SPACE	SCYTHE	RESENTMENT
FORLORN	CAPRICIOUS	SERENADED	VAPORS	AMBUSHED
TORMENTED	MUSSED	CASCADE	TAUT	SKEINS

Esperanza Rising Vocabulary

BUOYED	STAGNANT	ERUPTED	YEARNING	BROODED
DEMEANOR	PLAITED	PREOCCUPIED	PERSISTENT	RELUCTANTLY
EXTRAVAGANT	INDEBTED	FREE SPACE	SQUALOR	SUSCEPTIBLE
ANTICIPATED	RECLINING	WEARY	WILTED	MARVELED
MAKESHIFT	DOTING	OPTIMISM	RESOUNDING	FRANTICALLY

Esperanza Rising Vocabulary

DEBRIS	REGAL	WEARY	FRANTICALLY	MESMERIZED
MUSSED	AMBUSHED	RENEGADES	MENACING	DESPONDENT
RESOUNDING	DEMEANOR	FREE SPACE	PERSISTENT	TAUT
BEREFT	YEARNING	MONOTONOUS	VAPORS	SERENADED
TORMENTED	JALOPY	PUNGENT	CORDIAL	GINGERLY

Esperanza Rising Vocabulary

DWINDLED	COT	TORRENT	SCYTHE	PENETRATE
SQUALOR	SOLEMNLY	TAUNTING	FRAYED	SKEINS
ACCUSTOMED	MARVELED	FREE SPACE	RELUCTANTLY	VENOM
CAREENING	SUSCEPTIBLE	DEPORTATIONS	RETRIEVED	BUOYED
RECLINING	BESTOWED	SALVAGE	VALISE	BROODED

Esperanza Rising Vocabulary

SUSCEPTIBLE	FRANTICALLY	GINGERLY	DOTING	SUPPLENESS
COT	SQUALOR	VALISE	SERENADED	ESCORTED
DWINDLED	PERSISTENT	FREE SPACE	RENEGADES	DEVOUTLY
WEARY	VAPORS	INFURIATED	TAUNTING	DEBRIS
STAGNANT	SOLEMNLY	WILTED	SKEINS	AMBUSHED

Esperanza Rising Vocabulary

SHRINE	EXTRAVAGANT	BROODED	BUOYED	RETRIEVED
PENETRATE	PREOCCUPIED	SPEWING	SALVAGE	INDEBTED
MAKESHIFT	MUSSED	FREE SPACE	RESENTMENT	YEARNING
COPE	FORLORN	CORRUPT	MARVELED	DEMEANOR
IMMUNIZED	MENACING	TAUT	VENOM	ANTICIPATED

Esperanza Rising Vocabulary

JALOPY	SPEWING	SQUALOR	PENETRATE	VALISE
ACCOSTING	SERENADED	SUPPLENESS	INFURIATED	UNDULATING
IMMUNIZED	MAKESHIFT	FREE SPACE	CASCADE	BESTOWED
RESENTMENT	RELUCTANTLY	SOLEMNLY	ACCUSTOMED	FRANTICALLY
TALLOW	PLAITED	COT	VAPORS	RELAPSE

Esperanza Rising Vocabulary

WEARY	BROODED	STAGNANT	ERUPTED	STRIKE
SUSCEPTIBLE	MESMERIZED	MENACING	RESOUNDING	BUOYED
INDEBTED	CAREENING	FREE SPACE	MONOTONOUS	TAUNTING
PREOCCUPIED	DEVOUTLY	PUNGENT	FORLORN	COPE
BEREFT	SALVAGE	SHRINE	MUSSED	SCYTHE

Esperanza Rising Vocabulary

DWINDLED	SUSCEPTIBLE	DEMEANOR	STRIKE	RELAPSE
DEBRIS	OPTIMISM	WEARY	INFURIATED	CORDIAL
SHRINE	ERUPTED	FREE SPACE	RETRIEVED	FRAYED
VAPORS	VALISE	GINGERLY	BESTOWED	ACCUSTOMED
MENACING	BUOYED	FRANTICALLY	RIVETED	MAKESHIFT

Esperanza Rising Vocabulary

IMMUNIZED	SERENADED	MESMERIZED	EXTRAVAGANT	BROODED
MONOTONOUS	RESOUNDING	VENOM	CAPRICIOUS	COPE
JALOPY	MARVELED	FREE SPACE	TALLOW	SQUALOR
RECLINING	STAGNANT	RENEGADES	TAUT	RESENTMENT
PREOCCUPIED	TAUNTING	SOLEMNLY	CASCADE	SALVAGE

Esperanza Rising Vocabulary

SHRINE	SCORN	UNDULATING	WEARY	SKEINS
SPEWING	SCYTHE	MAKESHIFT	COPE	RETRIEVED
BEREFT	IMMUNIZED	FREE SPACE	SALVAGE	YEARNING
CONDOLENCES	AMBUSHED	RECLINING	BUOYED	ACCUSTOMED
RESOUNDING	MUSSED	WILTED	FORLORN	DEMEANOR

Esperanza Rising Vocabulary

VALISE	OPTIMISM	TALLOW	VAPORS	MONOTONOUS
VENOM	BESTOWED	PLAITED	DEVOUTLY	DEPORTATIONS
BROODED	INDEBTED	FREE SPACE	CORDIAL	TORMENTED
FRANTICALLY	MARVELED	RELUCTANTLY	DOTING	TAUNTING
DWINDLED	PENETRATE	ACCOSTING	CAREENING	CAPRICIOUS

Esperanza Rising Vocabulary

ANTICIPATED	RETRIEVED	SERENADED	DOTING	MAKESHIFT
DWINDLED	SQUALOR	DEPORTATIONS	BESTOWED	SUSCEPTIBLE
IMMUNIZED	UNDULATING	FREE SPACE	WEARY	STAGNANT
COT	PERSISTENT	TAUNTING	AMBUSHED	ESCORTED
DESPONDENT	INFURIATED	INTENT	VENOM	FORLORN

Esperanza Rising Vocabulary

CAREENING	SCYTHE	CASCADE	SHRINE	MONOTONOUS
ACCUSTOMED	STRIKE	SUPPLENESS	CORDIAL	TORMENTED
TAUT	SPEWING	FREE SPACE	TALLOW	INDEBTED
RESENTMENT	PUNGENT	RIVETED	COPE	PENETRATE
DROWSY	MENACING	PREOCCUPIED	REGAL	RECLINING

www.ingramcontent.com/pod-product-compliance
Lightning Source LLC
Chambersburg PA
CBHW081452070526
44586CB00019B/2321